Dr Justin Coulson and his wife, Kylie, have been married since the late 1990s and they are the parents of 6 daughters. At the time this book went to print, they are about to become grandparents for the first time.

Justin is the parenting expert and co-host of the hit Channel 9 TV show, *Parental Guidance*, and he and Kylie host Australia's #1 podcast on parenting and family life, *Happy Families*. Justin has written a number of parenting books, and speaks and consults about the intersection of psychology, family life, and wellbeing.

Find out more at happyfamilies.com.au

THE PARENTING REVOLUTION

Dr Justin Coulson

ABC BOOKS

Author's note

In the stories shared in this book, names and other details have been altered to protect the privacy of individuals, with the exceptions of those who gave permission to use real names and in examples drawn from my own family.

 The ABC 'Wave' device is a trademark of the Australian Broadcasting Corporation and is used under licence by HarperCollins*Publishers* Australia.

HarperCollins*Publishers*
Australia • Brazil • Canada • France • Germany • Holland • India
Italy • Japan • Mexico • New Zealand • Poland • Spain • Sweden
Switzerland • United Kingdom • United States of America

HarperCollins acknowledges the Traditional Custodians
of the land upon which we live and work, and pays respect
to Elders past and present.

First published in Australia in 2023
by HarperCollins*Publishers* Australia Pty Limited
Gadigal Country
Level 19, 201 Elizabeth Street, Sydney NSW 2000
ABN 36 009 913 517
harpercollins.com.au

A catalogue record for this book is available from the National Library of Australia

ISBN 978 0 7333 4251 6 (pbk)
ISBN 978 1 4607 1510 9 (ebook)

Cover design by Hazel Lam, HarperCollins Design Studio
Cover images by shutterstock.com
Back cover author photo by Liz Morris, Like a Boss Photography
Photograph on page i of Justin Coulson and his family © Tim Coulson
Typeset in Adobe Garamond Pro by Kirby Jones
Printed and bound by CPI Group (UK) Ltd, Croydon, CR0 4YY

Contents

Introduction

Let me save you a whole lot of hassle by giving you '*The Answer*' right up front. For the past 20 years I've spoken with parents who feel time poor, worn out, burnt out, and stressed out. If you're like them, you just want answers.

Now. So here it is on page one.

This is a book about great parenting and *what it takes to be a great parent*. Not a half-baked parent. Not a 'good-enough' parent. A *great* parent.

Research tells us we're investing more in our parenting than perhaps at any stage in the history of the world, but it's not working for us and it's not working for our children. Our parenting styles are stifling our kids. We're too controlling. We're too smothering, coddling, permissive and intrusive. Parenting is so intense! We're exhausted. But we push on because we want to be the best parents we can be for our children. They deserve it. How are we supposed to get parenting right and maintain our sanity?

Here's '*The Answer*': need-supportive parenting.

I know, I know. That's an answer that doesn't really tell you much, so let's break it down a little. Need-supportive parenting is the highest quality parenting I can describe for you. It consists of three essential elements. They're non-negotiable. They're critical to your ability to be a great parent. They tap into three irreducible and base psychological needs of your children.

The first of these elements is *positive and healthy involvement in your child's life.* This type of involvement satisfies your child's need to feel like she is seen, heard, and valued; that she is connected to you; that she matters; that she belongs somewhere*. In fact, if there is one factor that matters more than any other in parenting, resilience, wellbeing and anything to do with positive outcomes in our children's lives, it's this. The presence and involvement of one great human – safe, engaged, and involved – is unparalleled in its importance.

The second of these elements is *structure.* Here I'm referring to how we construct our children's lives, and the boundaries and limits that we develop (and *how* they are developed is every bit as important as *what* those limits are).

The third element is *autonomy support,* the linchpin of high-quality parenting. A linchpin is a locking pin. It's generally tiny. It is inserted through the end of an axle to prevent a wheel from sliding sideways. Without a linchpin, the wheels fall off! Autonomy support – encouraging children to act with a high level of personal choice (in developmentally appropriate ways) – is the element that ensures *involvement* is positive and *structures* are developed in healthy and functional ways.

This book is about autonomy support and the parenting style that works alongside it: need-supportive parenting. Autonomy support is *the* principle that, when practised, will change your parenting and your family for the better.

---

*   Throughout the book I'll alternate between she, he, and they pronouns to be as inclusive as possible for all children and families.

Over the following chapters, I will unpack need-supportive parenting systematically, explaining how it came about, how it compares with other approaches and how to implement it in your own family.

But first, a quick reality check.

Parenting and happiness

In Chapter Two of this book we'll explore the relationship between parenting and happiness thoroughly. For now, a quick summary: research keeps showing that having children is a reliable predictor of happiness *reduction*. We have kids and we begin to rate our lives as less satisfying, and other sources of happiness (like marital satisfaction) also drop.

Why?

You could probably put together a staggeringly long list if you tried, beginning with lost opportunities for romantic spontaneity shortly before baby's arrival and the need to begin scheduling romantic interludes for ever-diminishing amounts of time on an ever-decreasing schedule from that time forth. We are forced to unsubscribe from those last-minute airfare emails because an unplanned weekend away just became impossible. And once siblings arrive, the drama is multiplied. For example, we experience endless sleep deprivation and are forced to mediate apocalyptic relational challenges, like who gets to push the button for the elevator.

I'll briefly highlight three central reasons that explain this happiness drop once the kids arrive.

First, the constantly rising cost of having a child means the economics of child rearing are substantial. And it's not just the economic outlay on basics like food, clothing, and shelter. It's the sacrifice of professional opportunities. It's needing a bigger car or house. Rather than the convenient inner-city low-maintenance unit, you end up with a house in the 'burbs. Now there's additional expenditure on travel, the time it takes to mow lawns and maintain the place, the investment of hours into all that extra laundry and cleaning. Don't get me started on the cost of a family holiday versus a couple's getaway! And I haven't even begun to describe the emotional and psychological costs many parents experience. Kids cost.

The second reason is the cultural expectations around having a child. It seems as though just about every adult in the country has an opinion on how you should be raising your offspring, and the only thing they can agree on, apart from the importance of good parenting, is that *you're doing it wrong!* Those critical voices don't just come from outside us either. We really want to get parenting right. Desperately. That takes a toll. Perfectionism is associated with depression, anxiety, and burnout. Some of us approach parenting with a perfectionistic bent that hurts us and our kids.

Third, not only is parenting costly and impossible to get right. It's also exhausting. Relentlessly exhausting. In all the ways we can be exhausted, parenting will exhaust us.

Despite these and other challenges, a large portion of the population *wants* children. And when you ask kids about their perceived future, most of them say they want to be a mum or a dad. A large percentage of those who cannot have children are devastated at not being able to have them.

Why do we want kids so much? Why would we willingly engage in something that reduces happiness so reliably and be miserable when we can't? It seems irrational and entirely counterintuitive. And why do we resist this research, even though it has been well established since the late 1970s that having children is *not* associated with happiness? The cost-benefit analysis shows that the costs really are high relative to immediate, perceived benefits.

It's because parenting is a high-reward activity (or role). It's because a happy life and a meaningful or rewarding life are not the same thing. It's because of the inexplicable and unexplainable joy, pure and wholesome, that envelopes our heart when we look at that child – our creation – and bask in their laughter, their curiosity, their tender-hearted compassion, or the fact that they're finally asleep and peaceful. Holding that perfect little child, seeing your toddler overcome a challenge, watching your teenager help someone without realising you're watching … or just a quiet hug on a chilly morning with a child who you would give your life for; these things are incalculable rewards despite the tantrums, the exhaustion, the confusion … the cost. Children may not boost our happiness in those moment-to-moment psychological surveys. But they are a powerful source of meaning, awe, wonder, and joy.

We expect that parenting will be a major source of fulfilment. And for many of us it is, for one principal reason: *because it's so hard.* The short-term pain subsides. The meaning endures.

The power of hard

The general point here is that parenting is a tough gig and we've made it even tougher by operating our society the way that we do. This is why we read parenting books like this one: we want so desperately for someone to give us '*The Answer*', to *save* us, to make it easier. Many of us dream that some person, some philosophy or theory, some scientific advancement will spare us from the awful doubts and fears (or the sheer enormity of the task) so that family life can be like glossy parenting magazines make it seem. This illusion of problem-free parenting is encouraged by too many lousy self-help books, Instagram and TikTok gurus, or occasional well-meaning but unhelpful therapists or counsellors. We absorb what the headlines say and the photos display, and we feel incompetent, inadequate, unqualified.

But that simple, easy, blissful life where there is an answer to every question and challenge? It's not real. Parenting is a yoke. It's a burden. It's often unpleasant. Hard is where parenting exists. That is *why* it's so valuable and worthwhile.

Hard things grow us as people. They make us better. This elevates our sense of meaning and, eventually, our sense of happiness – because it elevates the quality of our relationships and connections. These connections are the most reliable predictor of happiness in the world. But it takes time, energy, focus, intention, and effort to be a great parent, and to practise the three principles of high-quality parenting.

Should we all just 'parent harder'?

My overwhelming concern for parents, however, isn't simply that parenting is hard. It's that our society's structures and systems are making it *harder*. There's a widespread belief – largely unspoken – that we have to 'parent harder' and more intensively than any previous generation, so that we can do it better. This belief is both untrue and unhelpful. This belief also amplifies the pressure too many parents are already struggling under as they stress about making the 'right' call on every decision so they can ensure their child's future welfare and success.

What is the best way forward? How do you become a need-supportive parent; someone who is involved, develops strong structures, and supports children's autonomy? In his paradigm-shifting book, *Beyond the Myth of Marital Happiness*, Dr Blaine Fowers emphasised a powerful point about the very best marriages. He stated:

'I have become convinced that strong marriages are built on the virtues or character strengths of the spouses. In other words, the best way to have a good marriage is to be a good person.'

Fowers is speaking about marriage, but we could easily substitute a few words and apply the idea to parenting. Slightly amended, the advice is this: 'The best way to [be] a good [parent] is to be a good person.'

Practising the principles I outline in this book doesn't provide any assurance of your cherished child choosing to listen, obey, and become the perfect son or daughter. It doesn't guarantee instant happiness. And it doesn't reduce the societal pressures to be the perfect parent, do it all without the support of a 'village', and protect your child effectively. But it does guarantee that *you* will become a better person, a better parent, and that, in time, your family will be happier.

Part 1:
The evolution of parenting

Parenting today is intense. There's an expectation that we are 'all in'. Fully invested. Completely committed.

But parenting hasn't always been like this. Over the centuries, the way we approach parenting has changed in dramatic – and not always helpful – ways. In this section, we review history's parenting errors. Be warned: it's frightening reading.

Unfortunately, while the specifics of how we parent have changed, we still get it wrong in our society-wide approach to raising kids. We'll look at why this is, with a focus on where our more advanced psychological research into families continues to fall short some of the time. We'll also examine why our current social media-driven fetishisation of parenting – our obsession with it – is not good for us, our children, our families or our society.

By the end of Part 1, you'll understand all of the modern parenting styles, including the unhelpful fads. You'll also be able to identify the parenting style that best describes your approach.

1

The dark past of parenting

Australians are slowly emerging from some of the longest Covid-19 lockdowns in the world as the final episode of series 1 of the hit reality TV show, *Parental Guidance*, moves toward its climax. Self-described 'tiger' parents, Kevin and Debbie – one of ten participating couples, each with different parenting styles – sit by a campfire in contemplative conversation. Over the past several weeks, they've completed various challenges with their two children, Mimi (aged 12) and Leo (aged 10). Each challenge has been designed to deliver to viewers maximum scrutiny on how parents *parent*. This 'wilderness adventure' is the last challenge for their family – and it's an especially difficult one for them all. Kevin and Debbie are city-dwellers who've never camped before. They're tired. They're a little bit emotional. It's been a long day that has tested their resolve and resilience.

Their conversation centres around their recent experiences participating in high-stakes TV challenges, navigating the unexpected with their children. As they watch the flames dance in the firepit and the soothing influence of nature mixes with the hard-won exhaustion of a day hiking and camping with their children, Debbie glances toward her husband. In a moment of tender vulnerability, Debbie softly asks Kevin, 'Am I a good mum?'

As Debbie gives voice to that question, I feel a lump in my throat. And as the television camera comes back to me in the studio, I realise I'm going to struggle to speak. Debbie has just asked the question that every intentional, loving parent asks every time they reflect on the way they are raising their children. It's a hard question to ask. The answer must be yes ... mustn't it?

What would it mean if the answer was no?

This question cuts to the very core of what, for many of us, feels like our ultimate purpose; our reason for being. *Am I a good parent?*

But mums and dads haven't always routinely asked themselves, 'Am I a good parent?' It's a surprisingly recent phenomenon.

It's parenting, but not as we know it

The *Oxford English Dictionary* did not recognise the word 'parenting' until 1918. 'Parenting' didn't show up in *Merriam-Webster* until 1958. 'Parent' had been a noun: a title, not a verb. The very idea that we – parents – would 'parent' our children didn't really take off until the 1970s. Until that period, the idea of parenting was not something on people's minds; just like the idea of 'husbanding' or 'wifing' isn't a thing. Nouns, not verbs.

In her book *Act Natural: A Cultural History of Misadventures in Parenting*, Jennifer Traig writes, '... a big part of the reason it wasn't called parenting is that for much of history, parents did so little of it. A cast of wet nurses, dry nurses, tutors, servants, slaves, clergy, older siblings, other relatives, and apprentice masters did the day-to-day labour.' She adds, 'The history of parenting is, in large part, a history of trying to get out of it.'

Top of Traig's list is the wet nurse. This is a woman paid to breastfeed and care for a child, sometimes for several years. While breastmilk sharing, as it is now known, occurred right around the Western world and was practised in Ancient Egypt and prior, for example to save the life of a child whose mother had died,[1] it was particularly common in 18th-century France. To avoid the inconvenience of parenting an infant and toddler, women of the elite would employ an in-house wet nurse; those with lower 'means' would send their babies away to poorer women to breastfeed and raise them. There was something of a trickledown effect in that, to maximise their earning potential, wet nurses in urban areas would then send *their* newborns to even poorer women in rural areas to be suckled. How common was this practice? To give one egregious example, records show that 17,000 of the 21,000 babies born in Paris in 1780 were sent off to wet nurses.[2] Only an estimated 1000 newborns were nursed by their own mothers that year.[3] Wet nursing was a business, and many parents were generally oblivious to negative impacts.[4,5]

Traig's review of the history of parents committing all manner of tragic acts – which is how we would view them today – is simply mind-boggling. Ample evidence shows that people often dealt with unwanted babies by 'exposing' the infant. In other words, the newborn was discarded, like the junk some people leave on the street outside random neighbours' homes. By some estimates, this occurred for 20 to 40 per cent of all births in major centres such as Rome, just two millennia ago.

Another practice that dates back centuries is swaddling, or tightly wrapping babies in blankets and/or cloth bands, at least in part to prevent them from moving. True, a swaddled baby often feels safer. We still swaddle today, albeit in a modified way. Weighted blankets are also popular for the feelings of comfort and security they provide. But swaddling wasn't just for comfort. A moving child was inconvenient, plus there were reasonable fears that a baby or toddler might injure herself or disappear if she could move of her own accord. By immobilising her limbs, safety and convenience concerns were catered for.[6] Swaddling could take considerable time, and so once swaddled, a child might well be cocooned for the day, often lying in her own filth until the swaddling was undone in the evening. Tying children up in some form of restraint was an almost universal parenting practice, with Romans continuing until around two months of age (although Plato records it as being two years!).

Ideas about disciplining children have gone through some astonishing phases. In the deeply religious Geneva of the time of theologian John Calvin (1509–64), for example, authoritarian rule by parents was total. If a child was rebellious, it could literally be a capital offence. In J.M.V. Audin's *History of the Life, Works, and Doctrines of John Calvin*, it's recorded that a young girl who had insulted her mother was 'kept confined, fed on bread and water, and obliged to express her repentance publicly in the church', and that a 'peasant boy who had called his mother a devil, and flung a stone at her was publicly whipped and suspended by his arms to a gallows as a sign that he deserved death, and was only spared on account of his youth'.[7]

Calvin is widely regarded (at least among Christians) as an important reformer and thinker. Nevertheless, his ideas about parenting were overwhelmingly authoritarian, as were the ideas of other well-known and highly regarded church and political leaders of that era. The prevailing religious view was that humanity – and particularly children – was depraved, fallen, and in desperate need of saving. Unquestioning obedience was the only path to salvation. Concern for the souls of children was the principal matter.

A final point on discipline. In a chapter of *Foundations of Psychohistory* called The Evolution of Childhood, Lloyd Demause stated:

> The evidence which I have collected on methods of disciplining children leads me to believe that a very large percentage of the children born prior to the eighteenth century were what would today be termed 'battered children'. Of over two hundred statements of advice on child-rearing prior to the eighteenth century which I have examined, most approved of beating children severely, and all allowed beating in varying circumstances ... Of the seventy children prior to the eighteenth century whose lives I have found, all were beaten except one.[8]

In case there is any confusion on the matter, Demause describes how children were hit: 'Beating instruments included whips of all kinds, including the cat-o'-nine-tails, shovels, canes, iron and wooden rods, bundles of sticks, the discipline (a whip made of small chains), and special school instruments like the flapper, which had a pear-shaped end and a round hole to raise blisters. Their comparative frequency of use may be indicated by the categories of the German schoolmaster who reckoned he had given 911,527 strokes with the stick, 124,000 lashes with the whip, 136,715 slaps with the hand, and 1,115,800 boxes on the ear. The beatings described in all of the sources I researched were generally severe (to our way of thinking), and almost always involved bruising and bloodying of the body. The punishment began early, and was a regular part of the child's life.'

Then there was the idea of children (and women) as property. A child was an economic resource. Depending on the social status of the family, a child could bring prestige or wealth through an advantageous marriage – a bride might bring the reward of a dowry or endowment. Most children were expected to contribute their labour to the household as soon as was practicable and earn a wage from a young age to contribute to the family's living. We've all heard stories of kids being sent down the mines or working in factories and sweatshops, or being sent off to work for employers to reduce the financial burden on families. Children were not well treated. At all.

But remember, 'parenting' wasn't really a thing. Nor was 'childhood'.

And so, while we appropriately find these accounts of parenting astounding, 'The past,' according to English novelist L.P. Hartley, 'is a foreign country: they do things differently there.'[9]

The ideas and anecdotes I've discussed are unfortunately generally reflective of the attitude of most parents of their times. The documented historical record offers ample evidence that these things really did happen and were neither uncommon, or surprising. (In too many places today, some of these practices still occur.) We may never really comprehend the way children were treated for much of history. Perhaps it's better that we don't.

The modernisation of parenting

The focus on child rearing sharpened through the mid-1700s during the Enlightenment. Thinkers like John Locke and Jean-Jacques Rousseau began to influence the way parents viewed their responsibilities to their children: they suggested that parents raise their children themselves rather than relying on anyone else. Ironically, Locke was not a father. And Rousseau – who famously wrote in his 1762 novel, *Émile*, 'What wisdom can you find that is greater than kindness?' – put all five of his children into foundling homes so he could concentrate on his writing.[10] Regardless of their parental inexperience or failings, these two men pointed parents towards greater involvement and even warmth with their children.

As the 1800s arrived, the belief (by now driven primarily by the American Puritans) that child rearing truly was the responsibility of parents became firmly embedded. Children were still seen as valuable only to the extent that they were economically useful, but things were beginning to shift. Sociologist Viviana Zelizer observed that, by the 1800s, children were now considered 'economically worthless but emotionally priceless'.[11]

Parenting in the 1900s

In the early 1900s psychology was born and psychologists began to offer opinions on child rearing. Surely life for children has been oodles better since psychology became an academic discipline and we've had science to inform our parenting?

Not necessarily. If we survey the past 100 years in Western culture, we may be taken aback at what's been considered reasonable behaviour for a parent. In the 1920s and '30s, for instance, people living in high-rise buildings in London affixed cages to their windows so their babies could benefit from fresh air and sunshine. Imagine an air-conditioning unit perched in a window. Now put a cage around it and fasten it to the exterior brick wall several floors up. Remove your imaginary aircon unit and stick your baby in that cage on a mat or towel so he can catch the breeze. How terrifying!

Two prominent commentators at around this time were Frederic Truby King, a Scotsman who became New Zealand's Director of Child Welfare; and the renowned 'father' of modern psychology, John B. Watson. They started talking about how to rear children with specific intention (without using the term 'parenting'). While nowhere near as austere as Calvin, both these men individually emphasised the moral authority of the parent. Children should be obedient, and they could be shaped by rewards and punishments. Authoritarian approaches were encouraged (because the only alternative, in their mind, was permissiveness). Child rearing (not parenting) was heavily routine-based.[12]

Such advice made quite a lot of sense. Health issues were rife. Antibiotics and modern medicine were unavailable. Parents weren't deeply absorbed in the intricacies of child development. So Truby King, John Watson and others emphasised physical and psychological health and exhorted parents to improve access to fresh air, good food and firm discipline. There's no doubt that this was an improvement over earlier practices. But a central tenet of this approach makes us shudder 100 years on: these experts cautioned against the 'dangers of too much mother love'. Watson, specifically, stated 'Won't you then remember when you are tempted to pet your child that mother love is a dangerous instrument? An instrument which may inflict a never healing wound, a wound which may make infancy unhappy, adolescence a nightmare, an instrument which may wreck your adult son or daughter's vocational future and their chances for marital happiness.'[13] Their positions fundamentally discouraged bonding with children.[14]

As the 20th century progressed, however, views about child rearing slowly began to change. This was likely due to the influence of people such as British psychologist John Bowlby and his attachment theory, which actively encouraged bonding with children. Unfortunately, not only did the parenting advice change, but it also became contradictory. Emerging science clashed with centuries-old practices. Inevitably, some parents and experts opted to cling to outdated customs, while others pushed for new ideas to take hold.

Parents began to compare notes. Norms shifted. Expectations for how parents should involve themselves in the act of parenting became more child-centric. This coincided with increased material prosperity following WWII. Mothers typically stayed home, with more time and money to spend on their children that ever before. Parents took on, and even sought, more and more responsibility for their children's happiness and life outcomes. This meant that education increased in value and academic pressures rose. Enrichment activities for children became more popular: no longer were swimming lessons and preschool education only for the wealthy. Parenting became a skill – a set of practices that mothers and fathers could develop, improve and leverage to foster personal fulfilment and success in life for their child. And parenting became a tool of comparison and judgment.

The modern parent

Studies indicate that since the 1990s, the pressure parents place on themselves has ratcheted right up. Parenting practice has become increasingly absorbing and exacting as parents attempt to 'get it right'. You might say we have fetishised parenting. Middle-class parents today are likely to optimise their children's environment so they can 'fulfill their potential'. We now put considerable effort into raising children to be 'successful' as they mature and grow, far greater than parents of two millenia, two centuries, or even two decades ago.

This places high and ever-intensifying demands on parents as well as children. We spend more money on our children than ever before. We spend more time with our children than ever before. We expect more of our children than ever before. And in many cases, we judge ourselves and *our* worth based on the outcomes of our children more than ever before. Parenting has not only become more resource intensive (primarily time and money), but it has also become a part of our identities. Social media has fed into this. Notably, the emergence of the mummy-blog universe – which has migrated from blogs to Facebook, and on to Instagram and TikTok in recent years – has led to parenting style labels being affixed when trend-conscious (or just trend-responsive) parents strive to show the world how connected they are to their kids. Common labels are attachment parents, helicopter parents, gentle parents, free-range parents, slow parents and nature parents, but there are so many others. We'll talk about those in Chapter 3.

The good news is that as scientific research has improved, so too has our parenting. It's now an established fact that our children do better when they have warm and involved parents who help provide structure that keeps them safe. The data show that in the West, most parents are looking after their little ones well; in some ways, perhaps better than ever. The majority of children are strong, healthy and enriched. In a 2021 study, Ana Okorn, a researcher at the Behavioural Science Institute in the Netherlands, found that when mothers and fathers are involved with and supportive of their toddlers, their children are less likely to act out aggressively or behave in challenging ways. They're also far less likely to have major emotional difficulties.[15] This finding is echoed by researchers worldwide for children at every age and stage of development. In other words, our recently developed focus on 'parenting' means we no longer cage our children or leave them exposed on the streets! Most parents in our society treat their children comparatively well and children are more likely to thrive as a result.

Running faster than our legs can carry us

The bad news? Parental burnout.

The never-ending pursuit of more and the relentless desire to better support our children is exhausting us. A 42-nation study of parental burnout, involving over 100 collaborating researchers, says parents around the globe are stressed.[16] In total, 17,409 parents responded to this questionnaire, and their answers showed that cultural values around parenting predicted who would be burnt-out and who wouldn't. Those from more affluent, individualistic countries were the most stressed about parenting. They were the ones (or perhaps I should say 'we' were the ones) who agreed to statements like:

> I feel completely run down by my role as a parent
> I tell myself I'm no longer the parent I used to be
> I do not enjoy being with my children

Reading these statements sounds depressing. Yet I speak, daily, with parents of children – from toddlers to teens – who confirm that the pressure of 'living up' to the expectations of society on parents is exhausting them. The impact of this intensive parenting is also affecting our kids. Anxiety is at record levels in our children, at least in part because we're ignoring the best science and pushing too hard. Suicide attempts and hospital presentation for suicidal ideation in children and youth is trending upwards in Australia and overseas at alarming levels.

Even though we take parenting seriously today, and even though we have decades of continually improving research to guide us, we can't really prepare ourselves for what parenting will require. There's an ocean of research that outlines how parents can raise their children well, but we are not taking advantage of it at a society-wide level. Instead, we are too tied to the past and our ineffective parenting history. And we are too tied to a vision of

1. The dark past of parenting

our child's 'success', which is also promoting unhealthy parenting practices that do not align with the best that science can offer.

This is where our challenge lies. We want to get things right. But what does 'right' mean? And how do we know when we're getting it right? Parenting needs a revolution.

Good parenting?

How do we identify whether we are a good parent? Do we look at how our child is turning out and use that as our metric? But turning out when? Now? In five years? Once they're an adult? If they are the dux of kindy or prep, are we nailing it? If they're one of the good-looking, popular ones, does that mean we're good parents? Or is that just a question of lucky genes? Sports star of the year at school? Academically gifted or musically or artistically talented? Good parenting? Good luck? Both?

Using a child's relative successes or failures in comparison to peers as a measure of whether we are or aren't good parents is unhelpful and unhealthy, but many of us look to them for signals that our parenting is on the right track; if we're doing well in the parenting stakes. But is how good you are at parenting even relevant to how your child turns out? What if your child has ADHD and, in spite of his genius mental ability, he has limited capacity to inhibit his behaviour and so doesn't fulfil his academic potential? And he's clumsy in social situations. You watch from a distance as he stumbles with his efforts to make friends. You know he has a beautiful heart; he's a gorgeous kid. He just can't seem to get it together. Does this mean you're not a good parent?

What if you've provided a nurturing environment, built trust, had all of the important conversations, been present ... and your child experiments with alcohol or other drugs, makes morally questionable choices or drops out of school to pursue his 'art' - and that 'art' is making YouTube videos or becoming a Twitch streamer for his 17 followers? (Those videos may end up being legitimate over time, but it can be really scary for a parent to experience our child trying to figure out if his chosen career path is viable, in real time.) Are you a good parent while your children are young and compliant, but once they're in their teens and making independent choices that conflict with your value system, are you now a bad parent? What if, at 15 years old, mental illness grips them with no warning after a seemingly perfect upbringing? How does that affect how you see yourself as a parent?

The science of being a 'good' parent

Two frameworks inform this book. Readers with psychology training will immediately recognise the 2 x 2 model of parenting styles, based on demandingness and responsiveness, whereby parents are categorised as authoritative, authoritarian, permissive, or disengaged. Researchers, including Diana Baumrind (in the 1960s) and Eleanor Maccoby and John Martin (in the 1990s), are the central figures in this work. We will explore this framework (which, for convenience, I will refer to as Diana Baumrind's work from this point forward) in practical detail throughout the book. The Self-Determination Theory framework also threads its way through these pages and forms the foundation of the practical advice given. This is our alternative guide to Baumrind's more famous but somewhat outdated model.

The Self-Determination Theory framework is going to improve your parenting in powerful ways. It goes far beyond the scientific advances made into parenting-style research built on Baumrind and those who extended her work (but we need to understand Baumrind and those who built on her legacy if we're to understand the past and present so we can move to a dynamic and positive future).

While science underpins everything in this book, what I'm offering in these pages isn't an academic treatise on parenting. It's more of an operating manual. I'm placing the practical advice – the art of parenting – front and centre so that you know what you should do. I want the recommendations to be easy to apply. But to really understand the application, there has to be some theoretical foundation.

The world has changed from what it was when we were kids. That means that some of the things we grapple with as parents are dissimilar to the things our parents were challenged by. Our children are facing challenges we never did. But this is a book about parenting and human behaviour principles that *don't* change, even if the context does. The ideas in this book are designed to take the weight off you and your child.

No 'right' way to parent

People consistently tell me, 'There's no one right way to parent.' Perhaps, but my response is twofold. First, there are plenty of 'wrong' ways to parent. The historical examples of child abuse earlier in the chapter are Exhibit A. We need to avoid behaviours that can harm our kids. Second, while there is no single pathway to follow, no single script to memorise, and no one 'right' decision for every situation, science does highlight:

- specific characteristics which are associated with the best outcomes in parenting, and

- specific principles which, when followed, are likely to lead to flourishing families and positive childhoods.

This book outlines the best way I know to get our parenting 'right', based on the highest quality science available combined with the experience of raising six of my own kids and helping innumerable parents with their children. The principles, strategies, and characteristics I discuss will be helpful for any parent trying to create greater harmony and love in their home, and raise strong, caring children. They're principles, strategies and characteristics designed to help us know that, regardless of how things turn out, we can confidently say, 'Yes, I'm a good parent' when we pause and reflect on that question.

But a deep puzzle remains. Is our desire to be 'good parents' driving us mad? If parenting matters so much, why does it so often feel hard and why does it so often make us miserable?

2

The 'impossible' profession

It appears we may have an impossible standard we are trying to live up to when it comes to our parenting. And it's not making us happy. In the introduction to this book, I briefly touched on the relationship between being a parent and feeling satisfied with life. This chapter explores this finding more deeply.

In December 2004, *Science*, one of the world's most prestigious scientific journals, published a research report that has become one of the most cited and best known parenting studies in psychology today.[1] The study found that mums experience more positive emotion when they are eating, shopping, talking with friends, or watching TV, than they did when caring for their children. The study generated global headlines. People were aghast. Isn't parenting supposed to light us up and bring us joy? How could it be that parents would rate other things more positively than being with their own children? Many studies have found that parenting reduces our happiness, but this is *the* study that grabbed people's attention.

Nobel-prizewinning psychologist and economist Daniel Kahneman was the lead author. He isn't a parenting researcher.

None of his four collaborators were parenting researchers either. The study wasn't even designed as a parenting study. So how is it that a study that wasn't about parenting became so central in conversations about parenting? Here's what actually happened:

Nine hundred and nine regular mums in Texas, each juggling work and family commitments, agreed to participate in a study about *life satisfaction* – not parenting. They completed a survey pack that asked them to construct a short diary of the previous day. 'Think of your day as a continuous series of scenes or episodes in a film,' they were told. 'Give each episode a brief name that will help you remember it (for example, 'commuting to work', or 'at lunch with B' ...). Write down the approximate times at which each episode began and ended. Where were you? Who were you with? How did you feel?'

Again, to be clear, the researchers weren't asking about parenting attitudes. They wanted to know how these women *felt* as they were going about a wide range of daily activities. It was only at the end of the experiment, as the data were being analysed, that the researchers made their discovery about parenting.

At the risk of losing you to sleep, the fridge, Netflix, or a child in need, I want you to take a look at this snapshot of data from the study. It's important, and I promise I won't get too far into the weeds. You can see the activities these participants engaged in that day, the degree to which they felt positively or negatively about them, and also how competent, impatient, and tired they felt as they did each of those activities. (Note that scores range from 0 = terrible to 6 = awesome.)

Activities	Positive	Negative	Competent	Impatient	Tired
Intimate Relations	5.10	0.36	4.57	0.74	3.09
Socialising	4.59	0.57	4.32	1.20	2.33
Relaxing	4.42	0.51	4.05	0.84	3.44
Pray/worship/meditate	4.35	0.59	4.45	1.04	2.95
Eating	4.34	0.59	4.12	0.95	2.55
Exercising	4.31	0.50	4.26	1.58	2.42
Watching TV	4.19	0.58	3.95	1.02	3.54
Shopping	3.95	0.74	4.26	2.08	2.66
Preparing Food	3.93	0.69	4.20	1.54	3.11
On the phone	3.92	0.85	4.35	1.92	2.92
Care of my children	3.86	0.91	4.19	1.95	3.56
Email/Computer stuff	3.81	0.80	4.57	1.93	2.62
Housework	3.73	0.77	4.23	2.11	3.40
Working	3.62	0.97	4.45	2.70	2.42
Commuting	3.43	0.89	4.09	2.60	2.75

What stands out to you here? Before we talk parenting, let's pay attention to a handful of basic but important things. If you've paused to look at the numbers, you might have noticed the following:

First, the most positive item in the list. On average, women scored their moments of intimacy that previous day as highly positive (thank goodness!), and they felt highly competent while engaging in those intimate moments (phew!). But did you notice how tired they were? The timing of the 10 pm nookie isn't serving anyone well. My guess is that the 5.10 out of 6 positivity rating would have jumped up to at least 5.70 if it happened earlier in the evening … if only the kids would get to bed on time.

Now on to the rest of the data. Like most people in our society, the participants of this study (educated, working, living in an affluent, major metropolitan city in the cultural West) felt positive more than they felt negative as they went about their daily lives. Even things that don't typically make people feel all that positive – like housework, working, and commuting – didn't leave them feeling overly negative. This accords with what positive psychology tells us: once we find our flow, we don't mind performing humdrum tasks. These participants reported that emotions while doing those activities were well below a 'peak' positive experience, but they didn't recall having a bad time doing them. Plus, for the most part they felt capable as they progressed through their day, except for watching TV, which ironically scored worst on competence, and was also the second-lowest activity on the 'tired' scale, behind caring for kids. The take-home message from that activity: screens don't rejuvenate our lives. As compelling as they are, we are better to stay off them.

The area we need to zero in on here is the parenting. The parents in this study ranked childcare as creating about the same amount of positivity in their lives as *housework*. It's one of the least positively rated activities on the entire list. And as I mentioned, parenting is associated with feeling tired: the participants felt even more tired in their parenting activities than they felt while watching TV.

Let's pause here for a moment. You're in a conversation with a close friend. She leans in and seeks reassurance that if she conveys a secret, you won't shame her. You laugh nervously, unsure of where this is going, and agree to withhold judgment. She cautiously confesses, 'I would rather watch TV, shop, or prepare a meal than take care of my kids.' You try to mask the shock on your face. Then she adds, 'In fact, if it was a choice between taking care of the kids or doing housework, I'd have to think about it before I could decide.' With exhausted exasperation she sighs, 'I am just so tired.'

Do you exhale and say 'Same here!', or do you look at her with disdain?

Are we *good* parents if we feel like parenting makes us feel negative? Is the data from the Kahneman study aberrant? Was this a subset of neglectful parents? And where do *you* rate looking after the kids on that scale of activities?

Do children make us miserable?

Since the 1980s, study after study after study has emphasised that happiness is *not* having kids.[2] We now have decades of well-documented evidence that marital (or partner) satisfaction drops for many people when a baby is brought into a relationship.[3] The studies also show that parent wellbeing often declines following the birth of a child and throughout their childhood. The effects can be long-lasting,[4] continuing even *after* the children leave home.[5] Here comes the kicker: the more children people have, the more likely the surveys will indicate lower wellbeing,[6] particularly with more than three children. I am not highlighting this because I want to talk you out of having children, or so that I can make you think you should be miserable if you aren't. You and I both know countless parents who are lit up with genuine delight as they raise their children. But raising kids is hard for the majority of us at least some of the time.

While thinking about parenting has changed a lot over time, we do know that parents in the past also struggled with their children.

Michel de Montaigne (1533–92), one of the leading philosophers of the French Renaissance, said of his children, 'I have not willingly suffered them to be brought up near me.'[7] This quote, more than any other, makes me laugh out loud. We've all had days (or weeks or months or years) where we would rather not have our children be brought up near us! In the previous chapter I mentioned Rousseau leaving his five children at an orphanage so he could spend more time writing. Even the Buddha named his son 'Burden'. How's that for a shot of self-esteem every time someone calls your name? 'Hey Burden, not like that. Like this.' (Fascinating sidebar: the Buddha left his family only a week after Burden was born so he could travel a path to enlightenment – without the kids.)

The famed father of psychoanalysis, Sigmund Freud, numbered education of children as one of the three 'impossible professions' (where the other two were governing nations and psychoanalysis[8]). He stated that raising and educating children was a role 'in which one can be sure beforehand of achieving unsatisfying results'.[9] In other words, you already know before you've started that you won't achieve the outcome you're seeking. In the late 1800s through to the early 1900s, mothers medicated their kids with cocaine- and opiate-spiked syrups so they could get through the day (and apparently quite a lot of mums took them as well – they were known as 'mother's little helper'. After WWII they were typically Valium and Librium)[10].

To understand a bit more about why parenting is utterly and in every way exhausting, impossibly heart-expanding, and achingly soul-stretching, we need to talk about modern research into parenting and happiness. The data probably show happiness declining for parents because raising children introduces hardship into our lives that we might not otherwise have to face. As stated in the introduction, it can be staggeringly expensive to raise a child, not to mention time-consuming, and physically and emotionally tiring. Many of our children encounter developmental, social, psychological, or neurological challenges as they get older. Some experience them all. These things wear us down.

Moment of truth

There's a less obvious explanation for why parenting is associated with unhappiness. It's deeply personal and it's the kind of thing we'd probably never say to another soul – even our life partner:

If we are honest with ourselves about our parenting, we know we don't measure up.

We want to be kind and calm, but we yell. We want to guide our children to play nicely together but they fight, and we snap. We want to give them great opportunities, but life is expensive, time is limited, and other children have needs too. Sometimes we have a child who is tricky, and we can't figure things out. We want to be the ideal parent we imagine everyone else is, but we can't ever be good enough. If being a 'good parent' matters to us, we are going to be driven to try harder and do more; to prove that we are the good parents we identify as. And we mostly cannot get there. That's why it's one of Freud's impossible challenges. Parenting creates an existential crisis as we contemplate how we're supposed to get it right and how we simply cannot.

Adding insult to injury, parenting might also make us miserable because we can't agree on how to do it. Parenting is ultimately about values, and when two people in a couple value things related to their children differently, it can be a recipe for conflict and unhappiness. Jennifer Senior, author of the bestselling *All Joy and No Fun: The Paradox of Modern Parenthood,* provides a glimpse as to why being a parent provides the perfect backdrop for relationship stress when she writes that children, 'more than money, more than work, more than in-laws, more than annoying personal habits, communication styles, leisure activities, commitment issues, bothersome friends, [and more than] sex'[11] become the basis of argument and conflict at home.

Conflict and kids go hand in hand for many couples. In my work with parents, I've heard arguments about parenting issues like:

- Why aren't they going to bed on time?

- Who said it was okay that they eat chocolate before 10 am (or before the age of three!)?

- Why do you keep giving in to him?

- I don't want the kids sleeping in our bed ... or in our bedroom.

- I don't think we should be sending them to that school. It's too expensive.

- You think she has a learning disorder? I think she's lazy. And no, we're not spending money on another psychologist!

- Why did you let him use the bath as a toilet?

- Do you really have to drink while you're pregnant?

- I don't like that you're letting the kids ride on the outside of the 4 x 4 when we're camping. It's so dangerous.

- In my day my dad would have given me a swift backhander and I never would have disrespected him again. We need to send that kid a message loud and clear. You're too soft on him.

When our children have additional needs (like ADHD, ODD, autism, and so on) such value clashes and parenting priority issues are amplified.

I highlight all of this to emphasise and acknowledge that parenting is exhausting physically, but it's also exhausting psychologically and emotionally. It's exhausting relationally. It puts pressure on us in ways that are hard to describe. And much of it is new to us as a society.

As society has shifted and parental expectations have intensified, current research increasingly shows that it's *normal* to be feeling tired and over it when you're interacting with your children – at least some of the time. It's *normal* to have conflict with a partner about how to deal with parenting questions – at least some of the time. It's *normal* to prefer watching a new show on your favourite streaming service, talking with a friend (or any random adult in a call centre), or pretty much anything really, over playing *another* game of Pokémon Go – at least some of the time! Research confirms that what you're feeling is almost universal. Parenting is often tedious, tiring, and taxing. The tools emphasised in this book will help you to reduce those feelings, but they won't eliminate them.

Children's irrationality, demandingness, and utter dependence guarantee that you'll always experience a level of ruin. No advice in any book can remove that reality.

Parenting makes life matter

But if parenting *is* so horribly hard, why do we say it's such a wonderful pleasure? There's a widespread belief – and expectation – in every culture in the world that children are a delight and a blessing, and that they 'should' make us happy. There are parents who shake their head in disbelief when I describe the research we've just considered. 'Oh no, that's not true for me,' they self-righteously (and earnestly) assert. 'I love playing with my kids and being with my kids and doing everything with and for my kids *all the time.*' Perhaps that's true. But for the rest of us?

The good news is that while parenting *is* hard for most of us, parents also enjoy moments of incredible delight. My academic research with a large sample of Australian families found that the more parents invested in parenting, the more likely it was that they would parent using an ideal parenting style, find pleasure in parenting and gain satisfaction from parenting, as well as experiencing a higher sense of meaning and satisfaction with life.[12] In a nutshell, they'd be happy – regardless of how many children they had. The icing on the cake came in a follow-up study where I found that when parents had these positive experiences, their children were more likely to be engaged in life, report positive outcomes, and thrive.[13]

What's really going on is this: when we are asked about the 'big picture' of parenting, we consider the transcendent experiences, the funny moments, and the flashes of perfection. But when we focus on the moment-to-moment difficulties of parenting, as the participants in the 2004 study did, our recollections of what it is to be a parent are harsher. And that shows up in the data that indicates parenting makes us miserable. Our *moment-to-moment* satisfaction is not the same as our *overall* satisfaction when it comes to parenting.

Consider this from a career perspective. A criminal court judge might express high satisfaction with her work overall, but not feel particularly enthused about life when dealing with an unrepentant murderer. A gardener might feel overwhelmed when he looks at an overgrown yard that needs maintenance, and he might feel frustration during the heat of the day when his fuel tank empties, his whipper snipper runs out of trimming line, and the insects are biting. But he likely feels tremendous satisfaction when he surveys his completed labours. Similarly, a parent could experience all kinds of negative emotions and challenging upheavals with a child over the course of one day, but still feel deeply satisfied with parenting (and a little relieved) as her child drifts off to peaceful sleep.

Personal factors may predict how happy we are as parents

In the Kahneman study quoted at the start of this chapter, you'll recall that participants had to rate how they were feeling as they participated in their daily activities, and they also described *when* those activities took place. The times of day during which the mothers in this study were most irritable and tired were early in the morning and later in the afternoon and evening. This next point is critical.

All of the mums in this sample had been at paid employment on the day of data collection: none were home-based. Surely this is going to affect the quality of interaction between parent and child and consequently how the mums feel about being parents. Being tired and stressed is not associated with feeling positive about much at all, let alone parenting. Moreover, when do we interact with our children? If your family is like most families, it will be early in the morning and later in the afternoon and evening. The pressure is on and emotional fuel tanks are depleted. These are the primary times we get to be with our kids: when we're not at our best and neither are they.

As smart as the Kahneman study was, we must be careful of the conclusions we draw from it. Does parenting make us miserable? Maybe. Maybe not. But you know what does make us miserable? Trying to parent – or pretty much do anything – when we are exhausted and the kids are exhausted. *That* is horrible.

Research shows that other factors are associated with the joy you experience in parenting: the quality of the relationship you share with your partner, or indeed whether you are partnered, any financial stress you are experiencing, your work satisfaction, how many children you're raising and any additional needs they have, parenting support you receive from parents or in-laws, mental health issues (for you or your partner), and so on. The list is long.

Ultimately, the headlines from studies such as Kahneman's give us little to go on if we want a clear answer about the relationship between children and happiness. Defining happiness is complex.

Are we talking about feeling vital and alive? Or experiencing purpose, meaning, and contentment? Are we talking about now? Or while the children are fighting? Or perhaps just after they've gone down for a nap? Moreover, the details of these studies leave us wanting. Parenting is complex. Life is complex. The contradictory and limited nature of the several studies that continue to paint parenting in a negative light fail to demonstrate the meaningful ways that our children shape our lives and experiences. For all of the reasons parenting upsets our otherwise well-ordered lives, there are deep and moving reasons it improves and builds us. Children improve our lives in some ways. They compromise and undermine them in others. Capturing the complexity of family life in a one-day study, where a small number of mums mentally recreated the previous day and offered approximations of how positively and negatively they'd felt while they completed the daily necessities, is nearly impossible, and shamefully reductionist. Yet this study is held up as one that informs much of psychology on how parenting works.

The conversation, however, is valuable. It forces us to pause and consider how we engage with our children each day. It causes us to contemplate how we can structure our habits to improve the way we interact and the way we grow. It compels us to consider the way we raise them – more specifically, it prompts us to consider our parenting style.

3 The ever-shifting goalposts of 'good' parenting

'Are you saying my dad wasn't a good dad?' A farmer was standing at the back of the seminar room, a reluctant participant in my evening workshop in regional South Australia. He'd left work early to hear what the 'parenting expert' (me) had to say, but the truth is he was only there to appease his wife. It was easy to see he didn't like what he was hearing, and now he'd decided to take me on. When he spoke, the challenge rested heavily on me like the sunburn on his cracked, parched lips.

I stalled as I considered how to respond to his question. 'Can you tell me about your dad a little? Did he act in a way that was different to what we've been discussing?'

The farmer responded, 'I was scared of my dad. I still am. But because I was so scared, I never put a foot wrong. And when I did, I made sure he wouldn't find out. I don't want my kids to go down the wrong path, so I'm going to keep them as scared of me as I was of my dad. Are you saying he did the wrong thing? 'Cos I reckon he was a great dad.'

Working on the right questions

If parenting wasn't a 'thing' like it is today until at least the 1970s, and since it became a 'thing' many parents have been struggling under the weight of it, we must address and finesse what it means to be a good parent.

The idea of a 'good' parent gets us into trouble. The central reason? 'Good' means different things to different people. 'Good' is a value judgment. 'Good' tells us nothing helpful – only that the person saying things are good has decided that they are good, according to them. Chapter 1 is full of examples where parents behaved, in today's terms, unconscionably. But it would seem they believed there was nothing wrong with their parenting. If they thought about it at all, they likely felt that they were good parents; after all, they fed and clothed their kids and gave them a roof over their heads and a start in life. They showed them how to get along and contribute to the world. Surely that's good parenting? And in the highly religious climate of their day, their discipline was all about their concern for the eternal welfare of their child's soul! Surely, they might argue, that is not just good parenting. It's great parenting. The farmer above is another example. Here is a man who believed it was good that he feared his father because it kept him on the straight and narrow. (Although his admission that he became sneaky so he wouldn't get caught is revealing.)

Some parents consider themselves to be 'good' parents because they co-sleep with their children. These parents argue it helps with feelings of safety and attachment. Others feel it's 'good' parenting to have their child sleep in a separate room from day one. Parents who subscribe to this approach suggest it allows everyone to be well rested so they can be nice to one another the following day, and it teaches kids independence. I've met many parents who think it's 'good' parenting to push their children to excel academically, even if it means the kids miss out on recreational or social opportunities after school or on weekends because of tutoring commitments; those parents believe great grades and a potent work ethic will set their child up for success in life. Yet other parents have assured me it's 'good' parenting to reduce academic expectations so their children can enjoy childhood, participate in extracurricular activities, and have time to spend with family and friends. In a similar vein, some parents think it's vital their children do it all and have every opportunity so they can find their spark, their strength, or their joy. Others take the view that it's vital their children have unstructured downtime to enjoy childhood, and leave self-discovery for later in life. Each thinks their approach is 'good' parenting. One dad told me he felt it was 'good' that his 13-year-old had been absent from school for over 90 days across two terms because it meant more time in the ocean, concentrating on his future pro-surfing career.

Some parents are adamant it's 'good' to teach their children that Santa is real, while other parents think it's 'good' to tell the truth about fictional Christmas and Easter characters (and tooth fairies). Similarly, there are those who raise their children with religious faith and those who don't, and each argues their decision reflects a 'good' choice.

I've had conversations with parents who believe it's 'good' to teach sexual abstinence as the only sex education their children receive, and I've had conversations with parents who believe it's 'good' if their teenagers have sleepovers with a boyfriend or girlfriend so they can experiment and learn about their sexual desires in a safe place rather than in a car or at a party.

Cross-cultural examples make the question of 'good' even more vexing. In a traditional Spanish household, expect dinner to be served around 9 pm and the children to be awake and involved with their family until even later. Children in many Asian families also stay up late, though this is often less about fiesta with family and more about study for school. Given all we know about children's brain development and their need for sleep, is this good parenting? In Denmark, the Netherlands, and other Scandinavian countries, parents leave their babies asleep in their strollers *outside in the cold* while they go inside the cafe and eat. They maintain that the fresh air offers health benefits. When Lenore Skenazy, founder of the Free-Range Kids movement, revealed that she allowed her nine-year-old son to catch the New York subway home (it was only two stops), she was called 'the world's worst mum'. Yet it's commonplace for Japanese children as young as four or five to do the same thing, although usually with an older sibling (perhaps aged seven or eight). In Finland, kids don't start formal schooling and learning to read until the age of seven! So which parents are the 'good parents'?

A case study: Is this good parenting?

My favourite parenting story, set in the 1950s, comes from a TED talk by Arbinger Institute cofounder James Ferrell.[1] Ferrell describes how, after saving for years, a man buys a new car for the family. His old truck (ute) was rusty, unreliable, and badly in need of replacement, so the new car was a big deal. The man was a forestry worker and the family lived in the national park where he worked. The family home was situated on the high side of the road. Directly opposite the house, on the other side of the road, a sheer cliff dropped steeply to a canyon valley.

A short time after the dad brought the new car home, the teenage son asked if he might borrow the new car rather than driving the old truck that they'd kept as a spare for teaching the children to drive and for running errands. The boy was a good kid. He was responsible. He was willing to work. He had a track record of doing the right thing. Dad agreed and handed over the keys with a gentle reminder to 'go steady' while driving the new car. The boy was elated and ran to the vehicle, eager to pick up his date and show off the new wheels.

After driving about a minute down the road, the boy noticed that there was no fuel in the tank. Being a typical teenager, he had no cash for gas! He spun the car around, returned home, raced inside the house, and asked dad for some money so he could fill the tank. Dad was in the bedroom reading the paper. He obliged his son with some money and the boy dashed back out the front door to drive away. Only … the car wasn't there.

The boy sprinted down the driveway, crossed the road, and peered into the canyon, where smoke was rising from the completely wrecked car on the valley floor below. All he could surmise was that he'd left the handbrake off and the vehicle had rolled down the driveway, across the road, and over the cliff. He couldn't remember, but that was the only explanation. And now the car – his dad's new car that he'd saved so hard for – was a smouldering wreck at the bottom of the canyon. How could he tell his father? Forlorn, the boy walked back into the house, re-entered the bedroom, and stammered to his dad that the car was gone. His dad continued to read the paper. His son stood in silence. After a minute the father quietly replied, 'Well I guess you'll need to take the old truck on your date tonight instead.'

My question for you: is this father a 'good' parent?

As we progress deeper into this book, you'll see why I love this story, and why I feel this man was a 'good' dad.

Parent harder

We experience tension when we contemplate whether we are good parents. The reason for this tension is twofold.

First, set aside the fact that we've spent an entire chapter attempting to define 'good' in parenting, and we can't. Let's focus on 'good' as a goal. What does that mean? One of the best known strategies for setting goals is the SMART goal system. SMART goals require us to set a goal that is Specific, Measurable, Achievable, Relevant, and Timebound. So let's set a SMART goal to be a good parent. What does that look like?

Can we be specific? Let's agree that a good parent is loving. But what does loving look like? How can we be specific about the need to be loving? Perhaps we must avoid shouting, criticising, or hurting our child. But there's more to being loving than avoiding punitive parenting. A loving parent spends time listening, playing, and teaching their child. They invest in their child. And the list goes on. Suddenly it's strangely non-specific.

But it's also difficult to measure being loving. Kilograms lost on a fitness binge? Dollars saved towards that financial goal? We can calculate these things. Weight and dollars are objective realities and are easy to measure. Measuring how much love we've offered our child throughout the day is staggeringly subjective and probably unhelpful.

Specific is hard to define. Measurable is a mess. Once we consider 'achievable', we know we're in further trouble. Being a loving parent all the time is disappointingly unachievable. We can't do it. We get angry, or flustered, or stressed. We miscommunicate (more on this later).

At least the 'relevant' concept fits. Being loving may not be specific, measurable, or achievable, but there is no doubt that it's relevant to the family context.

As for 'timebound', how long do you plan on being a loving parent? This is a goal that you never really get to the end of. It lasts at least a couple of decades, but really it's a lifelong pursuit.

The second reason we feel tension around the subjective self-judgment of whether we are or aren't good parents is because, in our heart of hearts, *we know we're not.* Even the very best among us wishes we could be better. We eviscerate ourselves for losing our temper, for our impatience, and for our cruel criticism. We consider all the amazingly perfect parents we see in our social media feeds – and even in real life – and wonder why we can't be like them (forgetting that even they aren't like that all the time).

The conversation about whether someone is a good parent or not must stop. It's unhelpful for us as individuals. It's unhealthy for our relationships with other parents. It promotes judgment and jealousy. And it undermines our capacity for true connection, our readiness to expose our vulnerability, and our willingness to ask for help. Instead, we keep pretending we're doing everything just right. We parent harder. We demand more, discipline more, and invest more – and we fall apart when we hope no one is watching.

Now, the truth. We are all good parents ... sometimes. And we are all bad parents ... sometimes. On average, much of the time we're mediocre parents.

The trouble is that this is a hard truth to accept. Perhaps that's why many of us behave like ducks: we make it appear like we're gliding along when, below the surface, we're paddling furiously just trying to be 'good enough' parents.

Over the course of my career, as parenting has become more of a pressured pursuit, I've noticed that too many of us look to external measures as validation that we 'are enough'. And so we might push our children to attain higher grades, speak another language, play representative sport, or display their brilliance; not so they can find delight, but so they can 'fulfil their potential' and we can look like we are fabulous parents. (Note, there's nothing intrinsically wrong with children achieving outward signs of success, unless we are the ones driving it, rather than them.) But parenting harder isn't going to help us be better parents. Intensive parenting practices (which we'll discuss in the next chapter) are only adding fuel to the parenting-perfection fire. And we're losing sight of the process in pursuit of the perfect outcome.

Some more truth: perfection isn't what matters when it comes to parenting. Perfection is impossible. But even the outcome isn't what matters in parenting, because the process is too long and the endzone keeps moving. Parenting is not just a process. It's a role. Think about your parents. If they're alive, then in some ways they still parent you now.

So am I a good parent?

Tiger mum Debbie, who we met in Chapter 1 on the set of TV show *Parental Guidance*, was essentially asking the same question we are discussing here. She pushed her children hard so they could succeed. Debbie wasn't a one-dimensional character whose ego needed boosting. But she was, in part, driving her children towards excellence in music and academic pursuits because the culture around her had taught her that this is what it means to be a 'good' parent.

Yet the question she asked, 'Am I a good mum?', wasn't about whether her children had achieved enough. It wasn't about whether they'd accrued enough perfect grades, sat enough exams, and performed to expectations. It was a conversation about *her*. It was an acknowledgment that Debbie could never do it all; a recognition of her human frailty and inevitable failures as a mum. It was a plea for compassion and forgiveness from her husband, and an appeal for acceptance.

Parenting has changed so much over the centuries in part because of questions like Debbie's. Her question shows what we all want: to be good parents.

So how can we know if we're getting it right and becoming the kind of parent we're proud of? Is there any kind of map?

As it happens, there are a whole lot of maps that consider the parenting terrain from a range of perspectives. We might call those maps 'parenting styles'.

For many parents, their parenting style becomes a part of their identity. They mark the path, delineate directions around the various parenting obstacles we encounter, and promise to show us the way to be 'good' parents.

Is there a style that can do this best?

Modern parenting – a question of style

Whether previous generations knew it or not, they had a parenting style. They just weren't thinking about it and there weren't any names for what they were doing. That changed in the 1950s when social psychologist Earl Schaefer identified a set of three characteristics that could describe a parent's 'style'.

First, parenting style could be assessed on a continuum of acceptance versus rejection. Schaefer argued that some parents were incredibly accepting. Others were firmly rejecting, only looking fondly on their children when they complied with strict parental authority.

His second dimension was a continuum of firm versus lax behavioural control. Schaefer thought we could quantify parenting style through the manner in which authority was wielded (or eschewed).

Schaefer's third parenting dimension was a continuum built around psychological autonomy vs psychological control. He saw some parents giving their children lots of support in determining their own decisions and values. Other children experienced high levels of psychological control from parents who not only demanded behavioural compliance but expected their children to do as they were told or there would be 'consequences'.

This early work by Schaefer set the stage for a true parenting science to develop, informing parents of how their interactions with their children were associated with life outcomes.

In the 1960s, the woman who would become one of the world's most influential parenting-styles researcher, Diana Baumrind, built on Schaefer's groundbreaking work and labelled these dimensions responsiveness, demandingness, and autonomy.[1] Baumrind's theorising and experimentation is at the core of almost everything most professionals consider when it comes to parenting. Responsiveness and demandingness are the aspects most often discussed, while autonomy often disappears into the ether. But the central point for now is that, with Baumrind's research, categorisation became a reality. We could now identify what kind of parent we were, and label the parenting of those around us.

We all love a label

Since the 1960s, parenting research has blossomed. But parenting's big push into mainstream conversation lagged, building slowly through the 70s and 80s. Through the decades, the concept of parenting styles has developed academically (through the work of Schaefer, Baumrind, and many others), but also through the media. Each style is labelled based on where the intensification dial is turned up.

The ubiquity of the internet and social media has launched a parenting-styles explosion. Today, a quick search on the internet highlights the handful of scientifically validated parenting styles. But for some light entertainment you can also find out which Disney parenting style you practice.[2] (You can guess that Pocahontas might be a free-range parent.) Harry Potter fans will be delighted to know that their Hogwarts house can be indicative of their parenting pattern.[3] And for the corporate/management type, you can even learn how your Myers-Briggs type[4] relates to the kind of parent you'll be.[5]

What is a parenting style?

A parenting style is the cluster of habits and pattern of behaviours that a parent relies on in their parenting. It's that simple. Some parents are highly strung with high expectations. That's their style. Some parents are laissez-faire, completely relaxed, and generally uninvolved. Some parents are completely Type A, hyper-competitive, positive parents.

The media LOVES parenting styles. They're not so interested in the science. They just like the labels. They've embraced tiger, helicopter, and free-range parents. But these have been embellished and added to in creative and delightful ways. For example, the *Washington Post* republished a *We are Teachers* article in 2022 describing jackhammer parents; loud, relentless, destructive, and powered by fear.[6] That sparked a humorous *New Yorker* article by Jay Martel where parenting styles ran wild. There was discussion of leaf-blower parents who are 'very loud and aggressive. They don't actually deal with stuff so much as dramatically blow it around so that someone else will clean it up'. The air-fryer parent is either 'completely shut down or blasting intense heat, causing a protective crust to form around their children. These parents are considered healthier, since they don't use conventional methods, but end up being just as bad for you as everyone else'. The iPhone 6 parents are 'old, sluggish, and often slow on the uptake, although sometimes more reliable than more up-to-date parents, despite being quirky and often cracked'. And my personal favourite, the Tesla parent, who tends to be 'quiet, attractive, and ostensibly better for the world, but loathed by other parents for their sanctimoniousness.'[7]

Over the next few pages we'll review the most well known of these media-driven popular parenting styles.[8] (The academically oriented Baumrind styles are coming up in the next chapter, after the fun stuff.)

Based on Schaefer's 1950s characteristics, we'll assess each of these styles by turning the dial up or down on three areas:

- how involved, accepting and responsive the parent is

- how structured, firm and demanding the parent is, and

- how supportive of autonomy versus how psychologically controlling the parent is.[9]

I'll begin each section with a quick rating (non-scientific) of that style.

Helicopter parenting

Involved: 9 out of 10
Structured: 9 out of 10
Autonomy supportive: 5 out of 10

This is one of the very few 'popular' parenting styles that's crossed over from a media-driven idea to something defined and studied in academic research. And it was one of the earliest parenting styles to be popularised – meaning most people are familiar with the concept of a parent who constantly hovers over a child: supervising, intruding, 'helping', and governing most of the child's life and decisions. Helicopter parenting is one of the most intensive parenting styles a parent can choose. And it's on the rise.

When a parent consistently does for a child what that child can developmentally do for themselves, that parent is helicoptering. But helicopter parenting is not only defined by coddling and overprotective tendencies. The more intense helicopter parents also try to manage their children's social lives, direct their academic lives, pack their out-of-school hours with enrichment opportunities, and go above and beyond to ensure their child's safety at all times and in all things and in all places.

The idea of a helicopter parent has always been pejorative. It was first coined by child psychotherapist Haim Ginott in his 1969 classic, *Between Parent and Teenager*, in which he depicts a boy complaining that his mother was restricting his autonomy by hovering over him like a helicopter. But the term really took off and flew (if you'll pardon that awful pun) in the early 2000s, when university lecturers and administrators noticed 'helicopter parents' who were doing everything for their young adult children. They were waking them up for classes, calling lecturers and tutors to ask for assignment extensions, complaining about the grades their children were receiving, and controlling their children's lives, even though those children were now adults.

Helicopter parenting isn't universally seen as negative though, and some parents wear the title with pride. Their children are often high achievers. They're always on time and well prepared. The parents always know where their children are, who they're with, and what they're doing. Helicopter parents tend to be highly supportive.

One reason for parental endorsement of helicopter parenting is that, when your child needs help, you feel like you're a great parent when you help them. Did your child forget to take a lunchbox, homework, or a library book to school? Jump in the car and deliver the item. We feel like 'good' parents when we help them out of a tough spot. Helping your child is rewarding for you as a parent. But there may be times where it runs counter to what is best for their development. Because parents are instinctively 'just helping' rather than deliberately adopting an overly attentive style, many helicopter parents don't even know that they are helicopter parents.

A 2019 University of Michigan study called *Failure to Launch* suggested that about one quarter of parents in a major US survey acknowledged that they were the main barrier to their teen's independence, because of their helicoptering tendencies.[10] And the reason? It's easier to do things ourselves than to ask the kids to figure things out. And because controlling parents override their children's autonomy, some research indicates that children often rebel against helicopter parents. Helicopter parenting has other drawbacks. Some helicopter parents feel worn down by all of the supervising, controlling, liaising, organising, and monitoring, but some studies indicate that developmentally unreasonable over-involvement in children's lives reduces a child's motivation to do anything, undermines autonomy, trust and self-efficacy (they don't believe in themselves), and inhibits children's capacity to own and solve their own problems.[11] There's also some evidence that helicoptering can cause long-term mental health problems for kids. They tend to be shielded from the natural consequences of their decisions and can even engage in what psychologists call *learned helplessness* (which means they give up when things get tough, and expect someone else to come to the rescue).

Just as I completed a draft of this book, some compelling new research landed showing that helicopter parents also tend to support paternalistic social policies.[12] For example, helicopter parents were more likely than other parents to endorse statements such as 'I believe it is the government's job to protect its citizens from engaging in unhealthy eating behaviours', and also believe it is the responsibility of an employer to ensure its employees are saving for retirement, or a doctor's responsibility to limit drug addiction by refusing to prescribe repeated pain medication. The carryover of control may reflect something deeper than a political ideology. It may represent an anxiety about the world and a belief that people cannot govern themselves. If we as parents possess anxiety about the world and mistrust the people around us, is it any wonder that we would feel a profound need to control our children's lives?

Tiger parenting

Involved: 10 out of 10
Structured: 10 out of 10
Autonomy supportive: 2 out of 10

The next best-known parenting style, tiger parenting, was popularised by Yale Law School professor Amy Chua. Her controversial 2011 memoir, *Battle Hymn of the Tiger Mother*, in which she writes of the differences between Western and Chinese parents, was widely received as the ultimate tiger-parent manifesto. This is another example of the intensification of parenting – often to unhealthy extremes.

Tiger parenting is highly authoritarian; meaning parents use threats, shame, and ostracism to discipline and motivate. Children are expected to work hard and perform at an exceptional level in their academic and artistic pursuits. Obedience is not optional. Parents emphasise achievement and they drive their children hard to attain success.

Children raised under a tiger regime tend to do amazingly well, perhaps influenced by cultural expectations along with parenting technique. Ideally, they develop deep levels of self-discipline through the endless drilling, practising and studying they're required to complete.

However, various researchers have questioned whether this kind of self-discipline is healthy or effective. Some suggest that children of tiger parents aren't intrinsically motivated: they're not working hard because they want to, but because they feel it's what they must do to earn their parents' love. It's been found that when this happens the child can unconsciously adopt the attitudes of others (their parents) and fail to live life in a way that is authentic and true to themselves. Their sense of identity is stymied. They may also feel a compulsion to continually try to measure up. When this occurs, children may experience poor psychological outcomes.

Research highlights that this parenting does *not* create child prodigies. Instead, it's associated with alienation from parents, child depressive symptoms, psychological maladjustment, and high levels of academic pressure.[13]

Free-range parenting

Involved: 6 out of 10
Structured: 2 out of 10
Autonomy supportive: 8 out of 10

I get the sense that parenting, up until around the 1970s, was mostly free-range parenting. (Either that or it was neglectful, but I think we can be generous and give our forebears the benefit of the doubt here.) And – my bias is evident here – if I had to pick a style out of all the *pop-culture* parenting styles, it would be this one. Free-range parenting is less intensive that many of the other parenting styles, which is why I favour it against most of the others described in this chapter, and it is generally quite need-supportive.

In Chapter 3 I referred to Lenore Skenazy, a New York-based journalist and the founder of the Free-Range Kids movement. In 2008 she wrote an article titled, 'Why I Let My 9-Year-Old Ride the Subway Alone', and discussions about her parenting went viral. If you've ever ridden a New York subway you can probably understand how her article led to Skenazy being labelled the world's worst mum.

When I interviewed Skenazy for the *Happy Families* podcast, she reassured me, however, that her nine-year-old only travelled two stops on his maiden solo subway voyage. He'd made the same journey with his parents countless times before. He made the request to try it out on his own, much to his mother's terror. While Lenore and her husband were apprehensive, they didn't want to coddle their son. They talked with him about what to do, how to do it, and what to do if something happened. And he did it, successfully. As a result of the subsequent parent-shaming she endured, Skenazy launched the Free-Range movement as a protest against the bubble-wrapped, cotton-woolling of children as typified by helicopter parenting.

But what exactly is free-range parenting? How do we make sure we don't cross the line in terms of endangering our children or neglecting them? After all, there are laws about leaving kids alone at home and failing to provide appropriate supervision. Kids don't raise themselves!

According to Skenazy, free-range parenting fights 'the belief that our children are in constant danger from creeps, kidnapping, germs, grades, flashers, frustration, failure, baby snatchers, bugs, bullies, men, sleepovers and/or the perils of a non-organic grape'.[14] Skenazy wisely still believes in safety: in helmets, lifejackets, airbags, and seatbelts. The free-range approach is not about throwing caution to the wind – and our children to the wolves. Free-range parents have limits for their children. But they also believe in independence. As Skenazy says, children, like chickens, deserve a life outside the cage. Therefore free-range parents engage with their children to help them develop the skills they need to discover their own boundaries, which means plenty of unsupervised play (both indoors and outdoors), lots of independence (which is earned as children demonstrate competence and capability), and a recognition that being afraid for children's safety is generally not helpful.

Free-range parenting hasn't been well studied. What few research findings I could read on the topic suggest that children reared with this style of parenting tend to be resilient in the face of adversity, and they grow up to be happy adults.[15]

Attachment parenting

Involved: 10 out of 10
Structured: 4 out of 10
Autonomy supportive: 6 out of 10

Attachment parenting was popularised in the 1980s by American paediatrician William Sears and his wife, Martha. The Sears argued that our busy modern lives and the awful advice from parenting 'experts' (as well as our own selfishness) disconnect us from our children, and the best way to achieve the critically important 'secure attachment' our children need to thrive is through an intensive attachment process. This involves the mother being connected to her child as much as possible through babywearing, breastfeeding, bed-sharing with baby (or at the very least, bedroom-sharing), and being ultra-responsive to every need that the child has. The focus, in line with the 'attachment theory' writings of Sir Richard Bowlby, (building on the work of his father, John Bowlby), is to create continuous care. That is, constant attention day and night, seven days a week and 365 days a year. It is hyper-intensive, particularly during the very early years (though many attachment parents would disagree and condemn me for saying so), with the central focus being closeness that facilitates emotional regulation for the child and bonding between caregiver and child.

Is attachment parenting a style we should adopt if we want to be good parents? First, it's only possible in the early stages of a child's life. We can't wear our eight-year-olds. But there's a further consideration. Alan Sroufe, a developmental psychologist at the Institute for Child Development at the University of Minnesota, has studied the attachment relationship between parent and child for over 40 years. Sroufe is a veritable icon when it comes to child development and attachment. He states that 'these [attachment parenting principles] are all fine things, but they're not the essential things. There is no evidence that they are predictive of a secure attachment.'[16] Sroufe gives the example of breastfeeding, which is a central element of attachment parenting and is believed to foster high levels of emotional responsiveness. A parent who's exhausted, insensitive to her child, and generally non-responsive will promote an insecure attachment even if she's breastfeeding. But a mum who is bottle-feeding while connecting, cooing, and engaging warmly with her child will be creating a secure attachment, despite bottle-feeding being less desirable according to this parenting style.

The science is settled when it comes to attachment: it is wholly positive, and research findings support the link between emotional responsiveness and secure attachment; also that breastfeeding and keeping children close align with good maternal bonding. Still there are many shades of grey. It isn't necessary to be 100 per cent attentive to every whimper from a baby. That would be exhausting, and could teach a child to become overly dependent on parents.

And life has a tendency to disrupt even the best laid plans; it's been found that even in a secure relationship, misattunements can occur close to 70 per cent of the time.[17]

Misattunement doesn't mean a parent is ignoring or harming a baby. It means there's a mismatch in emotional synchrony or responsiveness between the mother and the child. Maybe mum thinks the child is tired but the little guy is hungry, or uncomfortable because the edge of his disposable nappy is cutting into his leg in an awkward way.

None of Sroufe's observations is an argument against any of the attachment practices or, heaven forbid, a recommendation for parental neglect. The reality is that attachment parenting is a style that has co-opted a scientifically based concept (secure attachment) and aligned it with a number of practices that seem good, make sense, and are generally healthy ... but are not always feasible. Parents who cannot breastfeed or who are exhausted from co-sleeping and babywearing may become swallowed up in feelings of guilt and failure (or worried about judgment from others), when these practices do not, in and of themselves, guarantee the secure attachment the parent is trying to develop. The parents run the risk of exhausting themselves chasing an elusive parenting perfection that isn't necessary for secure attachment to occur.

In fact, all this effort may impede that attachment. For the record, I love all of the individual practices and encourage them where mum is capable and the practices feel good, authentic, and within reach. How wonderful to be so close to your baby so much of the time. But if the cost is a mother's mental and physical health, perhaps we can turn down the involvement dial a bit.

It's entirely possible that nothing matters more for a well balanced, flourishing life than the attachment relationship a child shares with his or her parents. The data shows that children with a strong and secure attachment to their parents experience a greater sense of agency, better emotional regulation, higher self-esteem, better coping under stress, closer friendships in middle childhood, better coordination of friendships and social groups in adolescence, more trusting and positive romantic relationships in adulthood, greater social competence, more leadership qualities, and happier and better relationships with parents and siblings.[18] This is a big deal. It's just that 'attachment parenting' as a pop parenting style doesn't guarantee the secure relationship that leads to these outcomes.

French parenting

Involved: 6 out of 10

Structured: 7 out of 10

Autonomy supportive: 5 out of 10

From this point forward, it becomes increasingly challenging to clearly identify the parenting styles we'll discuss. While helicopter, tiger, free-range, and attachment parenting styles have been discussed for years and have even been studied to varying degrees, the nouveau French style (and the remainder of the styles on this list) are loosely defined and exist primarily on social media and in mummy blogs or popular books.

French parenting has been popularised in response to Pamela Druckerman's book *Bringing up Bébé*. According to Druckerman, the French treat children more like adults-in-training than helpless babies who need someone to do everything for them. Their focus is on helping children develop competence, believing that this will naturally instil greater confidence. Those who have compared French parenting to more common parenting styles in the USA, UK, Canada, and Australia suggest that the French:

- tend not to praise their children

- know how to be involved but not obsessive or over-involved

- ensure children understand that adults need time away from the children

- don't give their children options at dinner; the kids simply eat what the adults are eating, even if it's snails

- demand good manners

- say 'no' and mean it

- follow the free-range parenting philosophy that the world is a safe enough place for children to live life fully.

No doubt there are plenty of French parents who don't adhere to this style of parenting. Nevertheless, Druckerman's review of parenting, based on her time and observations while living in Paris, has given rise to a style that generates regular talk and lots of attempts at replication (and it was even represented in Season 1 of *Parental Guidance*).

Lawnmower or snowplough parenting

Involved: 10 out of 10
Structured: 10 out of 10
Autonomy supportive: 2 out of 10

You might sometimes hear this referred to as bulldozer parenting. In this style, the parent is assertive in protecting their offspring from anything and everything that might be difficult. It's another highly intensive parenting style. These parents push all obstacles out of their child's way. They're the 'Karens' and 'Kevins' of the parenting world, making calls to ensure their child is invited to every birthday party, gets to sit next to their friend in class, and is captain of the sporting team. It's the helicopter parent dressed up as a Blackhawk attack chopper. Any obstacles are blown off the path so the child can have a trouble-free ride through childhood and adolescence. To paraphrase an African proverb, lawnmower parents prepare the road for their child rather than preparing their child for the road.

Lawnmower parents are often ultra-competitive. Bystanders can get the impression that lawnmower parents regard their child as special or too good to fail. I don't see it like this. I think these are parents who love their kids and want them to achieve all they can in life. Lawnmower parents might also say things like, 'I don't want them to have to go through the hard things I went through.' These are understandable motives that come from a tremendous desire to help, but they can undermine a child's chance at growth through adversity.

These parents tend to swing from authoritarianism ('I expect great things from you') to permissiveness ('But of course if you want to do that you can').

While there's no research on these blog-style categories, my suspicion is that the small number of children raised by lawnmower parents are likely to feel entitled. Very entitled. Not an attractive thing in any child, but particularly unpleasant to encounter in an adult.

Gentle parenting

Involved: 10 out of 10
Structured: 7 out of 10
Autonomy supportive: 7 out of 10

The biggest parenting 'fad' right now – and one of the most polarising – is gentle parenting. There are no academic studies on gentle parenting. It's simply too new. It's also fairly loosely defined. A TikTok search, or a quick Google, will reveal the various ways that gentle parenting is both defined and conflated with a range of other parenting styles; notably attachment parenting and permissive parenting. My observation is that it's unlike either of those styles – although when not done the way it's supposed to be done, gentle parenting can easily become one of those two (or both).

Gentle parenting is a mindset characterised by empathy, respect, understanding, and boundaries. Its strong focus on supporting autonomy in children earns it a thumbs-up from me. Even so, it's not the parenting style we're ultimately working towards in this book. It's close, but not quite there.

The foundation of gentle parenting is emotional attunement. Gentle parents work hard to be loving, compassionate, and in tune with their child's emotional state. They want to understand the reasons behind their child's behaviour, recognising that when a child is upset it's because of an unmet need. Gentle parents are therefore deeply invested in their child's emotional world, and practise emotion coaching, mindfulness, and other techniques to help their child understand and regulate big emotions effectively. Gentle parenting is a *very* intensive parenting style, and observers often mock it because parents appear to be at the mercy of their children's emotional state.

Gentle parents do not rush in and correct their children if they don't like what they're doing. Instead, they patiently pause, listen to their child, and then validate their feelings. In a sibling fight, for example, a gentle parent might say, 'So you're cranky and yelling because you feel as though your sister was mean by excluding you, and that upsets you.' This validation (known as emotion coaching) without immediate correction will ideally help a child feel safe and understood, and ultimately calm down. At this point in the interaction the parent will problem-solve with the child to determine the best way forward. The idea is that this approach enhances emotional intelligence, meaning that, as children mature, they become skilled at identifying and regulating their own emotions, and can work with other people and *their* emotions effectively.

Sarah Ockwell-Smith is the author of *The Gentle Parenting Book*. She says: 'Gentle parenting isn't really about using specific methods. It's about an ethos and completely changing the way you think. It's more a way of being than a way of doing. Approaching any and all parenting situations with empathy for the child and trying to understand the reasonings behind their behaviour, working together to change it positively and accepting what cannot be changed.'

Because of the intensive nature of gentle parenting, this can be a tiring and demanding parenting style. It requires a commitment to elevating your child's needs to a central priority, and the capacity to hold firm to boundaries while being patient, understanding, attuned, and … well, gentle.

It also requires parents to navigate the constant stares and judgments of others. Accusations of poor parenting are common, as is advice to be more assertive, which can be a challenge for gentle parents.

The parenting styles in practice

Before we conclude this review, let's take a brief – albeit slightly simplistic and caricatured – look at how parents in each of the parenting styles we've considered might respond to an 11-year-old child who wants to ride her bike to visit with a friend in the next suburb.

> **Helicopter parent:** 'Okay. But I want you to take your phone with you so I can track your progress, or Facetime and talk to me at each corner … Maybe I can send up the drone to follow you and I'll watch from above? I'll just call their mum to make sure they're watching out for you too.' [Child leaves and parent follows at a safe distance, just out of sight.]

Tiger parent: 'Are you kidding me? You're not ready for your piano exam. It's four months until you sit it. You have practice to do. And tutoring is tonight as well. You won't be going anywhere.'

Free range parent: 'Yeah, you bet. Do you know where you're going? And do you know what to do if you're worried or in trouble? Great … Have fun. Be home before it's dark, okay?'

Attachment parent: [Technically, attachment parenting applies only to infancy and toddler years.]

French parent: 'Sure. Of course. Just talk to their parent and make sure it suits them. Let us know if you need any help with arrangements. We'll see you for dinner, okay?'

Lawnmower/Snowplough/Bulldozer parent: 'Right. Just let me get my bike helmet and you can ride behind me so we make sure you get there safely.'

Gentle parent: 'You'd love to spend time with your friend, wouldn't you? And you'll feel so big and responsible if you can get there all on your own. How are you feeling about heading off? What can I do to help?'

And all the others

We could talk about slow parents, nature parents, dolphin parents, little emperor parents, and the various other styles we saw on Season 1 of *Parental Guidance*; the routine, disciplinarian, and strict parents. Season 2 pushed the parenting styles labels even further with outback, influencer, roadschool, American, stage, team, honest, and lighthouse parents.

While each of these styles plays with the dials of responsiveness, demandingness, and autonomy support to different degrees, ultimately they're variations on the four main parenting styles we'll be discussing over the next several chapters.

5

Is this the kind of parent I am?

The 1960s weren't just a time of social revolution: a scientific revolution occurred as well. In 1961, the first human was launched into space. In 1962, a patent was created for the first seatbelt to be used in cars (can you believe they didn't have seatbelts until the '60s?). In 1966, the first handheld calculator was invented. In '67, surgeons performed the first human-to-human heart transplant. The first computer mouse arrived in 1968, and man stepped onto the moon in 1969.

During this period, parenting practices shifted considerably too. The stern, strict parenting of previous decades was replaced by permissiveness and freedom (at a broad, population level). This really was the era of kids playing out in the street or park until the dinner bell rang or the sun sank below the horizon. Children played with dangerous toys, took exploratory risks, and lived that nostalgic, carefree existence that shows like *The Wonder Years* celebrate. Life had its challenges, and injustices that should not be ignored,but for a lot of children, growing up in the '60s warranted the romanticised notions we give it today.

Parenting, however, would change forever in this decade. Diana

Baumrind's categorisation of parenting styles revolutionised the way psychologists see parenting, and '60s parents brought ideas about responsiveness, demandingness and autonomy to their interactions with their children.

Baumrind's investigations started a wave of studies into how children turned out in relation to how their parents parented. What they found could be summarised as the Goldilocks Principle. If Goldilocks were to try each of Baumrind's parenting styles, the first one (authoritarian) would be too harsh, the second style (permissive) would be too soft, and the third style (authoritative) would be just right. A couple of decades later, two other researchers, Maccoby and Martin, added the fourth parenting style: disengaged. They made important advances that still inform parenting science today.

With the establishment of data showing how our parenting was associated with child outcomes throughout the '70s, '80s and '90s, adopting the right parenting style became seen as increasingly important.

What kind of parent are you?

While the path to improved parenting begins with self-awareness and self-examination, there are surprisingly few ways to identify our default parenting style. No one figured out how to *measure* or *assess* parenting styles until 1995, when researchers at Utah's Brigham Young University developed what is *still* the only peer-reviewed, reliable diagnostic tool[1] to help parents work out which of Baumrind's styles best matches how they parent.[2]

Over the next few pages, you'll be able to take the test and see what your parenting style is.[3] It's simple. Just rate how often you exhibit each behaviour with your child. The scoring scale is as follows:

I exhibit this behaviour:

1 = Never

2 = Once in a while

3 = About half of the time

4 = Very often

5 = Always

It's possible that no answer perfectly matches the way you respond most of the time. That's fine. Just go with the answer that seems closest to your typical response. Don't overthink it. The test asks a handful of questions that seem repetitive. That's just to make sure that all of the relevant aspects of each parenting style are being assessed.

(It might be fun to take the test a second time and score your partner on each of these questionnaire items. Then have them go through the questionnaire the same way: once answering for themselves, and once scoring you. You can compare scores and discuss how your perceptions of your own and one another's parenting styles are different and why.)

1   I am responsive to my child's feelings and needs.

2   I use physical punishment as a way of disciplining my child.

75

3   I take my child's desires into account before asking the child to do something.

4   When my child asks why he/she has to conform, I state: because I said so, or I am your parent and I want you to.

5   I explain to my child how I feel about the child's good and bad behaviour.

6   I spank when my child is disobedient.

7   I encourage my child to talk about his/her troubles.

8   I find it difficult to discipline my child.

9   I encourage my child to freely express himself/herself even when disagreeing with me.

10   I punish by taking privileges away from my child with little if any explanation.

11   I emphasise the reasons for rules.

12   I give comfort and understanding when my child is upset.

13   I yell or shout when my child misbehaves.

14   I give praise when my child is good.

15   I give in to my child when she/he causes a commotion about something.

16   I explode in anger towards my child.

17   I threaten my child with punishment more often than actually giving it.

18   I take into account my child's preferences in making plans for the family.

19   I grab my child when they are being disobedient.

20   I state punishments to my child but do not actually do them.

21   I show respect for my child's opinions by encouraging my child to express them.

22   I allow my child to give input into family rules.

23   I scold and criticise to make my child improve.

24   I spoil my child.

25   I give my child reasons why rules should be obeyed.

26   I use threats as punishment with little or no justification.

27   I share warm and intimate time together with my child.

28   I punish by putting my child off somewhere alone, with little if any explanation.

29   I help my child to understand the impact of behaviour by encouraging him/her to talk about the consequences of his/her own actions.

30   I scold or criticise when my child's behaviour doesn't meet my expectations.

31 I explain the consequences of his/her behaviour.

32 I slap my child when she/he misbehaves.

How to interpret your scores

Authoritative

There are three subscales in the authoritative scale. Your connection, regulation, and autonomy-granting are each measured. To score connection, add up your score for items 1, 7, 12, 14, and 27. Now divide by 5 to calculate your connection score. Write your score here _____ and if your partner is taking the same test, write their score here _____.

To work out your regulation score, add your responses to items 5, 11, 25, 29, and 31. Now divide by 5 to calculate your regulation score. Write your score here _____ and if your partner is taking the same test, write their score here _____.

To finalise your autonomy-granting outcome, add your answers to items 3, 9, 18, 21, and 22. Once again divide by 5 to calculate your autonomy-granting score. Write your score here _____ and if your partner is taking the same test, write their score here _____.

Finally, to obtain an overall authoritative parenting score, add up the total of all 15 items, and divide by 15. Write your authoritative parenting score here _____ and if your partner is taking the same test, write their score here _____.

Authoritarian

As with the authoritative category, there are three subscales within the authoritarian scale. They are known as physical coercion, verbal hostility, and non-reasoning/punitive parenting scales. To calculate your physical coercion score, go through the same process. Sum your scores for items 2, 6, 19, and 32. This time, divide by 4 to get your overall score for physical coercion. Write your score here _____ and if your partner is taking the same test, write their score here _____.

The same process applies for verbal hostility. Total your scores for items 13, 16, 23, and 30, divide by four, and write your score for verbal hostility here _____ and if your partner is taking the same test, write their score here _____.

The items to add for the non-reasoning/punitive parenting subscale are items 4, 10, 26, and 28. Once you've divided that total by 4, write your score here _____ and if your partner is taking the same test, write their score here _____.

The last thing to do now is obtain an overall authoritarian parenting score, which means you'll add all 12 of those questionnaire items, and take the average by dividing by 12. Write your authoritarian parenting score here _____ and if your partner is taking the same test, write their score here _____.

Permissive

The final subscale is measuring how indulgent and permissive we are. Add up the final five items: 8, 15, 17, 20, and 24. Divide your total by 5. This gives you an overall permissive parenting score.

Write your score here _____ and if your partner is taking the same test, write their score here _____.

Compare your three scores. The higher you scored in any one dimension, the more you tend towards that style of parenting. Most people score highest on authoritative parenting. This is partly because these parenting behaviours are socially desirable in most cultures, while behaviours in the other dimensions are not.

Let's now look at how we can better understand each of these parenting styles and see how each style affects children. As you read, consider your interactions with your own children, recognising what is similar or different in these styles from the way you parent. It can also be useful to consider how you were raised. These memories can help you recognise patterns that have carried over from the way your parents raised you to the way you raise your child.

The authoritative parent

Most researchers and practitioners judge authoritative parents as the 'gold standard' in parenting.[4] Authoritative parents balance three things:

1 warmth and nurture (through love and support, which researchers call responsiveness)

2 demands (through limits, boundaries, and expectations, which researchers call demandingness), and

3 support for a child's freedom to make choices (which is known as autonomy support).

Here's how the model is depicted:

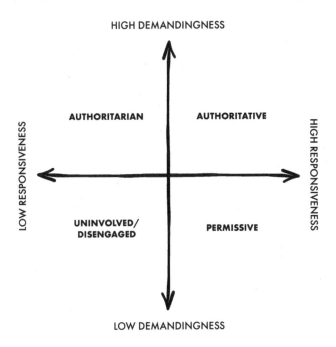

This is a challenging balance to strike, but authoritative parents strive to be consistent in:

- talking about challenges and difficulties the child experiences

- offering comfort when a child is upset, even if they 'caused' the upset themselves

- recognising a child's 'negative' emotions as a chance for connection

- providing reasons for rules

- explaining consequences of decisions and challenging behaviours (without a heavy-handed approach on negative sanctions)

- inviting the child to share their emotional state

- respecting the child's emotions

- encouraging a child to recognise how their behaviour affects others

- showing respect for a child's opinions by encouraging them to share ideas

- allowing a child to have input into decisions and rules

- taking a child's preferences into account before asking them to do something

Decades of research tells us that on all measures, children who experience authoritative parenting are better adapted and functional than those who experience authoritarian or permissive parenting. They usually regulate their emotions better than children raised with other styles and manage their own behaviour better too. As a result, they'll often:

- perform better at school

- enjoy better quality relationships

- be effective with skills like self-control

- have higher self-esteem

As they move into adolescence, these children are at reduced risk of internalising behaviour (such as depression and anxiety) and of externalising behaviour (such as conduct disorder, ADHD, and violent, aggressive, or delinquent behaviour). They're less likely to engage in drug use or sexual activity. These are the kids who become independent and self-reliant, but also know how to have positive relationships with others.

The authoritarian parent

Authoritarian parents tend to focus less on warmth, nurture, and support, and are more likely to emphasise limits and discipline/ punishment. This may include physical coercion, verbal expressions of hostility, or a punitive approach that makes children 'pay' so they'll 'learn their lesson'. Authoritarian parents will usually be found:

- using physical punishment to 'discipline'

- threatening, coercing, and using other punitive approaches to obtain compliance from their child

- yelling, scolding, and criticising

- removing privileges from a child, often with little in the way of explanation

- using time out (forcible isolation), often with little explanation

- relying on the 'my way or the highway' approach to reinforce the idea that it's 'my house, my rules'

Authoritarian parents don't allow much autonomy for their children and, while they certainly love their children, they don't usually show a lot of warmth towards them. Many authoritarian parents really just want one thing: compliance. After all, life is far less complicated when kids are obedient.

Studies show that children whose parents are authoritarian are no more compliant and obedient (except when they're being watched) than other kids. Researchers have found that children raised in this environment, even by well-meaning parents, are at increased likelihood of disruptive, aggressive, defiant, or antisocial behaviour. Authoritarian parenting is associated with greater risk of adolescent risk-taking, alcohol and other drug use (and abuse), delinquent behaviour, sexual promiscuity, and more. Teens who are raised this way are at increased risk of social exclusion, are likely to bully, and are at risk of anxiety, depression, and low self-esteem. They also often struggle with problem-solving and creativity tasks at school.

The permissive parent

Permissive parents tend to avoid confrontation and conflict with their children. They're not boundary setters, and let the children find their own limits. Permissive parents want their children to feel good and figure things out for themselves. And they definitely want their children to love them, lots. As a result, they'll typically be high on warmth and supportiveness, but will be less likely to encourage effective boundary setting and compliance with limits. Parents who fall into the permissive category are usually likely to:

- be inclined towards spoiling their child

- be easily persuaded to give in

- ignore behaviour that isn't in line with usual standards in society (or in most people's homes)

- be inconsistent in the way they establish limits, often letting their children get away with things even if limits were previously established

- be uncomfortable with any form of discipline or conversation about limits

Permissive parents protect their children from the worst outcomes of 'no limits' by remaining warm and nurturing. This is their saving grace. But their reluctance to develop and maintain limits with their children is associated with a range of challenging outcomes. Children raised this way tend to have relatively high self-esteem, and they'll often be reasonably resourceful and creative. Some studies suggest, however, that these children struggle to control their impulses, stay focused, manage their moods, and execute plans. This lack of planning and forethought may help explain why these kids are at risk of ignoring rules, being low in self-control, drinking alcohol or using drugs (as teens), watching too much TV or using screens excessively, and so forth. But ... it depends on the closeness of the relationship between parent and child. Warm, nurturing relationships can buffer these negative outcomes.

Interpret with caution

It's important to approach any psychological measurement tool with care, and that applies to this self-examination. Few people will fit into one box neatly. Instead, it's likely you'll be a little bit of each style.

It's also possible to play with the questionnaire: you might parent more or less in a particular style depending on the time of day. For example, consider how you parent at 3.30 Saturday afternoon when everyone is relaxed, fed, and playing in the park or on the sand at the beach, compared to 8.15 Tuesday night when bedtime was 45 minutes ago but the kids are still running around the house and you're exhausted. Even though you're scoring yourself on a scale of 1 through 5 based on how often you exhibit those behaviours as an average, you could play it out as an average response to the children at night, in the morning, or on weekends.

Hopefully, along with looking at where parenting has come from and why, I've convinced you of the merits of authoritative parenting. From here on, we can get into the nitty gritty of effective parenting.

A lot of water has gone under the bridge since Baumrind and other's work. For example, there have been significant changes in community attitudes towards hitting children – something Baumrind and other behaviourists supported in the context of an authoritative relationship. Moreover, parenting style 'types' feel judgmental and unhelpful. And they're not practical either.

Over the next chapters, I'm going to invite you to see parenting anew. Many of the changes in parenting style I'll share may seem like subtle shifts, but they're the kinds of shift that allow us to learn to be better parents and raise our children with minimum regret.

As mentioned earlier, many of the rewards of parenting come from doing hard things. In *Think Again*, Adam Grant, a Wharton business professor, asserts that 'a hallmark of wisdom is knowing when it's time to abandon some of your most treasured tools – and some of the most cherished parts of your identity.'[5] Prepare to be challenged. I promise you, it will be worth it.

Part 2:
The future of parenting

If you completed the questionnaire in the previous chapter, you've probably categorised yourself as a particular kind of parent. You might feel satisfied. Perhaps you're nailing it. Or … maybe you're noticing some elements of your parenting that don't feel quite right yet. Perhaps you discovered that your parenting is made up of a bit of this style and a bit of that style. It's not surprising if some days we're authoritarian tigers and other days we're too exhausted to be anything but permissive free-rangers.

Many parents recognise that they swing like a pendulum from permissive to authoritarian depending on how hungry or angry or lonely or tired or stressed they are. Don't get too tied to any of the parenting styles we've reviewed thus far. There's one parenting style still to unpack. I've saved the best for last.

We're about to move beyond the past of parenting – including authoritative parenting – to dig deep into the parenting style that helps children thrive and flourish best. In Part 2, we'll explore the basic psychological needs that our children have, and the elements and practices of high-quality parenting.

Chapter 6 will explore our children's basic psychological needs. Chapter 7 will outline how these needs should be supported and how we can best do this. Chapters 8 through 10 will pull apart each of the elements of high-quality parenting so we can create environments that help our children flourish.

This section is the very heart of what matters most in parenting. This is where we begin to turn all of those things we thought we knew about parenting on their head and move towards a future of parenting that is revolutionary.

Children's basic psychological needs

Academic conferences are a requirement of scholarly university life. A lapsed academic, William Deresiewicz, laments, 'Oh, the conferences. You fly across the country to sit in airless ballrooms, scented with the odour of professional futility, listening to airless talks.'[1] My experience matches his. While it sounds like staggering snobbery to complain about rubbing shoulders with peers in various amazing global locations, conferences actually *are* largely uninspiring events ... except, for me, in one instance. I met Ed Deci and Richard Ryan, these two giants of the psychology world, at a Self-Determination Theory academic conference a couple of years prior to Covid-19 disrupting all our lives. The location: Victoria, Vancouver Island, British Columbia. There wasn't the faintest whiff of professional futility; attending this conference was like breathing pure oxygen.

By then in his late 70s, Edward Deci is a tall, soft-spoken man. Warm and generous in his demeanour, I found Deci to be a scientist's scientist. His statements were firm in relation to his subject matter, but he retained a tentativeness and humility about the numerous scientific breakthroughs he has helped bring about.

His collaborator, Richard Ryan, is just over a decade younger. An ebullient and compelling speaker, quick-witted and humorous, his words conveyed thoughtful conviction. His encyclopaedic knowledge of decades of experiments was striking. In his address to the conference attendees, Ryan explained with precision how scientific discoveries have pointed to how we can best live life, and how best to raise our children. The most significant and foundational insight from these decades of research: we have clear evidence that when *basic psychological needs* are supported, people do well and want to do better.

Let's put this into parenting talk. Our children will be most inclined (motivated) to act in ways that facilitate flourishing when *we* create an environment that supports their basic psychological needs. In the terms these researchers use, parents are looking to create a 'need-supportive environment'; hence the concept of 'need-supportive parenting'.

'Need-supportive environments facilitate innate growth tendencies,' according to Professor Ryan. 'And at this point we have overwhelming evidence for three basic psychological needs.' Ryan explained that environments which support a sense of (i) relatedness, (ii) competence, and (iii) autonomy are the kinds of environments that are ideal.

In relation to parenting, we create our environment at the broadest level by choosing a city, suburb, street, and home to live in. The macro environment is a tremendous contributor to the extent that children have meaningful relationships with friends and extended family (to support their relatedness need), are able to navigate their way to the park, school, the shops, or other meaningful places, and have access to swimming lessons, music and art, and so on (to support their competence need), and can move safely from one place to another (to support their autonomy need).[2]

At the micro level, where we focus only on what we do as parents, need-supportive parenting – the kind that incorporates parental *involvement*, effective development of *structures*, and *autonomy support* – is exactly the kind of parenting that provides the support for those three basic psychological needs.

Let's explore these needs and what they mean for our parenting.

Relatedness

It's 1938. Researchers at Harvard University recruit 268 undergraduate students to participate in a long-term study. It becomes the longest running psychology study in the history of the world. It also becomes one of the most important, because it offers us a deep insight into the power of relationships when wellbeing is our focus.

Few women attended university in the pre-WWII era, so *The Study of Adult Development* at Harvard Medical School (known as the 'Grant Study' after one of the original researchers on the project), began with men only.[3] The goal of the study: follow these men and observe their lives, measuring *everything*, to understand who will flourish and who will fail. The men were interviewed regularly, took questionnaires consistently, had their IQ tested, blood analysed, body parts (including intimate areas) measured, handwriting analysed, and more. Information was obtained about their mental and physical health, the quality of their relationships, career experience, and even retirement. It was all in the name of understanding success and optimising life. Over time, the researchers expanded the study to include the spouses and children of the men being researched. And they also recruited just over 450 Boston inner-city youth from the 'working class' to provide socioeconomic diversity to the data.[4] The study included some extremely successful men, including one who later became the President of the United States of America: John F. Kennedy.[5]

What did the researchers find after collecting all of this data for all of these decades? A 2017 quote from the *Harvard Gazette* summarises the findings of the 80-year research project concisely:

> Close relationships, more than money or fame, are what
> keep people happy throughout their lives … Those ties
> protect people from life's discontents, help to delay mental
> and physical decline, and are better predictors of long
> and happy lives than social class, IQ, or even genes. That
> finding proved true across the board among both the
> Harvard men and the inner-city participants.[6]

The Grant Study found that, regardless of their baseline economic status (and whether they were the rich Harvard men or the inner-city Boston participants), those who grew up having warm, engaged connections with their parents earned more (as adults) than those who had less close relationships with their parents. They experienced greater happiness and life satisfaction. Support for relatedness needs continued to have a positive impact into adulthood too. When in an environment that supported adult connections (such as connecting positively with their spouse in marriage), people had less emotional difficulty. They had fewer cognitive challenges (such as dementia). They experienced less physical pain. The quality of their social connections and involvement with loved ones was associated with lower levels of physical and psychological disease. When relatedness needs are supported through loving and meaningful connection, people experience better life outcomes. As summarised by George Vaillant, who was the caretaker and lead researcher on the Grant Study for several decades, 'Happiness is love. Full stop.'

Our economy is built on dollars. Just as the dollar is the currency that drives our economy, connection is the currency that drives our relationships. An economy without dollars is dead. A relationship without relatedness and connection is too.

What does relatedness look like in practice? In the middle of a winter's afternoon, as I was working on this book, my then eight-year-old daughter had a breathtaking tantrum. We all have our moments, often because we're overwhelmed, exhausted, hungry, or just plain irritable. This particular child is still learning to navigate her big emotions. Over time I've learned that when she's emotionally elevated, she often needs space. Trying to talk or reason with her overstimulates her and escalates the tantrum further – which is neither in her interest nor mine. And while I'd love to have some 'time-in' with her so I can help her calm herself, this is something she sometimes rejects.

I offered to hug her and spend time with her to comfort her and guide her through her upset. She was mad and told me so. The words she shot across the room were 'LEAVE. ME. ALONE.' Each word was a complete sentence expelled at full volume, expending an entire breath.

I love my daughter. I want the very best for her. And I value my relationship with her. So … I gave her the space she needed.

After a few minutes passed, I approached her with a gentle suggestion. 'Want to play Skip Bo?' For context, I was in danger of missing my book deadline, I don't enjoy most games that come in a box (card games included), and I didn't want to be around an ornery child who had, moments before, been super rude. (Hey, I'm only human.) My daughter surprised me by saying 'Okay!' and I sacrificed half an hour of writing time to play a card game that I typically would avoid.

And yet that 30 minutes of involvement helped my daughter feel a sense of connection, belonging … relatedness. She knew she mattered. And it changed her. The remainder of our afternoon was peaceful because she felt safe in an environment that satisfied her need for relatedness. (I admit I enjoyed it too.)

Relatedness is demonstrated and experienced through warm, loving involvement that minimises control and judgment. This supportive connection increases security and safety. The more relatedness needs are supported, the more our children feel there is life in their relationships. Connection (feeling seen, heard, and valued) creates a sense of belonging; a feeling that 'I matter'. Our children thrive when they feel cared for, that they're significant in the life of someone else, and that they're integral to a group (like our family or friend network).

Need-supportive parenting satisfies our children's relatedness needs (as well as our own) by emphasising that element of high-quality parenting I referred to earlier: *involvement*. When we're involved in our children's lives we devote time to our children, investing attention to the relationship. We are caring and supportive, and we offer warmth, concern, and connection so our children feel seen, heard, and valued.

Competence

As a child I loved school. I had good friends. I performed reasonably well. My teachers were kind. It was a good place to be. As a teen, my parents put me into a school where I knew almost nobody. Their intentions were good. But my high school years saw a shift in my school attitude and experience. By Grade 8 I hated school. Loathed it. Deeply.

Perhaps it sounds hyperbolic, but at the time (and even on reflection), it felt as though high school destroyed me. I struggled to make friends. I felt lonely. In hindsight my teachers were remarkable people, but I felt so alone that my motivation plummeted and I stopped paying attention. Soon I was falling behind. Then I was failing. My parents were paying enormous fees for a fancy private school and I was squandering the education they were trying to give me. I hated being at *that* school (so I felt I had no autonomy). I had no friends (so my relatedness needs went unmet). And – no surprises here – because I had no relationships and no choices, I was putting in no effort, and I was failing (which meant my competence needs were thwarted).

At this point it was the late 1980s. My parents decided to take some time away from their retail furniture business and their six kids. My grandmother dutifully agreed to care for all of us while Mum and Dad travelled through Asia for two weeks. Picture the scene: I'm a school-hating teen with a bad attitude. My grandma sends me to my room to do my homework and I sit staring at my mathematics questions. It might as well be written in an ancient form of Nordic gibberish; maths has always felt indecipherable to me. I doodle on the A4 loose-leaf paper, drawing a picture of a wave. I feel good when I'm surfing. I surf with my friends (outside of school) whenever I can. I'm capable in the water. It feels so free. (There are those three needs being met ... no wonder I love surfing.) But the wave I've drawn isn't going to get me an 'A' on my next maths exam. I switch on the radio. I lose myself in music (and fantasise about my future career as a radio announcer, knowing that doing well at school is *not* a prerequisite for that line of work). Finally, I return to the textbook. It's as meaningless now as it was 20 minutes ago. And then ... my mind sparks. I know what to do about my maths homework.

About five minutes later my grandmother comes rushing into my bedroom, panic strewn across her face. Smoke from my metal rubbish can, in which the remains of my algebra are smouldering, has drifted through the house to where she's been giving my little sisters afternoon snacks. Fearing the house is on fire, Nan's followed her nose to my room; she sees my sense of academic competence turn to ash in the base of a rubbish bin.

I hated school. I felt so incompetent.

According to Deci and Ryan's Self-Determination Theory, competence is an essential need. If we can create an environment that supports our children's sense of competence, they're more likely to experience greater motivation and wellbeing. When they feel incompetent, motivation is sapped and wellbeing plummets. Kids say things like *I'm so stupid. This is so dumb. I hate this. Why do we have to go to school? No one cares about this, why are you making me do it?*

It's true that sometimes they are capable of doing the work that they're refusing to do. Ability is high but motivation is low. In that case, they're not whining because they can't. They're whining, instead, because they want control and we're taking that away. (That's our next need: autonomy.) But often they give up, throw the pen on the desk, burn their homework, walk away from the piano, or quit the sports team, because they feel like it's all too hard and they're not competent. Helping them to persist in these circumstances is tricky, but when the environment is need-supportive, they're more likely to be intrinsically motivated and to experience success.

What does a competence-supportive environment look like? A one-word explanation is that it looks like *scaffolding*. Scaffolding is a structure that supports the construction of a building. It's also a structure that supports the construction of our child's competence and the development of who they are as an individual.

Do you remember the last time you felt like you couldn't do something; a time when you were incompetent? If you don't normally run and I suggested that a quick 10-kilometre jog was exactly what you needed, would you be excited? Can you imagine jumping up and saying, 'You know what? I haven't run as far as the letterbox in a decade, but you're right! I need to run. It's going to be messy. I'll make a fool of myself. I probably can't run to the end of the street without getting a stitch or needing a knee replacement! But boy, I'm thrilled by this opportunity. Bring it on!'

Through their research, Deci and Ryan have determined that humans are intrinsically drawn to challenge and growth. But we're only drawn to it when we feel that we are choosing it (autonomy), it's tied to our relationships with others (relatedness), and we feel we can master it (competence).

What is your child's typical reaction when something is hard? Does your child retreat into herself so she can avoid the challenging situation she finds herself in? Does she retaliate and become angry and rebel? If so, she needs structure: scaffolding.

Creating an environment that supports competence means we set things up so that our children have a sense that, 'If I try at this, I might be able to figure it out.' It's the feeling of mastery that comes from knowing how to operate effectively in our environment. Sitting at the piano trying to play a new song can be overwhelming. Competence is thwarted. But when we provide scaffolding and structure – by suggesting something like, 'What about if you just play the left hand for the first line, and then the right hand, and then put them together?' – we operate in that zone where things are challenging but reachable. We support competence needs. Motivation lifts. Children attempt and persist. And then they achieve.

But competence is *easily* thwarted. It vanishes when challenges are too difficult, when negative feedback feels overwhelming, and when feelings of effectiveness are reduced because of comparison, competition, or not feeling 'enough'. There's a fine line between doing something too easily (which leads to boredom) and doing something too hard (which leads to frustration and quitting). Finding that 'zone of proximal development', where a child is on the cusp of doing the next hard thing, is the key.

Regrettably, children feel incompetent a lot of the time. At home parents point out failings and make demands. School increases the incompetence experience – a lot of kids spend most of their day feeling incompetent in the classroom. So much new content! All. The. Time. And then there are music teachers, sports coaches, and others who, with the best of intentions, spend a lot of time pointing out all the ways that their students are getting things wrong. 'Defend harder. Kick higher. Play that note softer. Try a little more.' While some children respond well, others hang their heads in defeat, thinking 'I'll never be good enough.'

Children who have additional needs (ADHD, ODD, autism, SPD etc.) require carefully targeted support for competence. That scaffolding and structure becomes a lifeline. The environment that supports their competence need is *everything*. Why? Because life often feels overwhelming. The feedback they hear most is that they can't do anything right. They may struggle socially, academically, physically, or cognitively. Parents dive in with the intention to fix things. But that attempt highlights, to the child, their incompetence. 'If I need fixing,' they think to themselves, 'does that mean I'm broken?' There's a flow-on effect too. Our efforts to fix can cascade into mistrust, puncturing relatedness. Then we become controlling, overriding autonomy.

Children's competence needs are hard to support consistently. Make no mistake, our children will benefit from our gentle guidance and encouragement when they feel incompetent and there are opportunities for improvement. But the way we guide them often matters more than the guidance itself. This is where the high-quality parenting element of structure becomes important. When we develop structures in our children's lives, we provide support for this competence need, and their motivation and wellbeing increase.

Autonomy

Let's say you're in a relationship with someone who's consistently correcting you. They tell you what to do even when you know what needs to be done. They tell you how to do it, when to do it, and what you didn't do right when you tried to do it. In other words, they're controlling you. How would you rate your experience of that person and that relationship?

This is life for most children.

Children *do* need someone to help them make safe, healthy decisions. Wise guidance from an authority figure isn't a luxury item: it's essential. But exert too much control and our kids start to push back. They rebel. Anyone who's raised a two-year-old or a three-nager knows how highly they prize their autonomy. Being in control is *everything*!

Why does force create resistance? Why do children react to being controlled? Because their frame of reference is being ignored. They can see something and don't understand why we can't see it too. They're having fun at the park, or they're exhausted from a big day. Perhaps they're in the middle of the best game they've ever played online, or a friend dumped them today and they feel low. Our controlling behaviours bump against their current context in uncomfortable ways. Need-supportive parents work hard to see the world through their child's frame of reference. Need-frustrating parents, who restrict rather than support autonomy, are perceived as authoritarian demand/command controllers. What does that feel like?

When children become defiant, we see their behaviour as autonomy assertion. A more charitable explanation is that they're struggling to regulate their emotions and need us to step into a higher-quality parenting response, where we see the world through their eyes, understand their challenge, and work together on solutions that are suitable for both of us.

Autonomy needs are best met when children feel like they're in charge of their own actions. They're regulating their behaviour without the need to be motivated by external factors such as rewards and punishments. The real difficulty with parenting – the hardest part of all – is helping our children to feel *intrinsically* motivated to make decisions that are in their best interest when they have a limited understanding of what *is* in their best interest! This is a challenge with toddlers, teens, and everything in between.

To appreciate how autonomy works as a need (for us and for our children), it helps to understand how motivation works. The table below shows a motivation continuum.[7]

Type of regulation	External	Introjected	Identified	Integrated	Internal
Where does it come from?	External	Somewhat external	Somewhat internal	Internal	Internal
Motivation source	Punishments and rewards	Ego; self-control	Recognising importance; conscious valuing	Congruence; consistent with self	Inherently satisfying. A reflection of personal identity

Whenever children are doing something because of the punishments and rewards that will follow, they're operating based on *external* motivation. They may be choosing to behave a certain way, but it's only because they want the 'goodie', or they're trying to avoid the horrible stuff. This is *not* a healthy or sustainable source of motivation. When we utilise extrinsic motivators consistently, our children aren't motivated to live well for any reason except what's in it for them. Once we're not there offering an incentive or threatening a punishment, the behaviour we want to see stops. This is the time-out, withdrawal of privileges, threats, bribes, yelling, smacking parenting style. This is the shallowest end of the motivation continuum.

Some people will say, 'Well, that's just how the world works.' It's true that some elements of our existence are like this. Such an environment is toxic; yet much of the world is precisely like this for our children, which perhaps offers a clue as to why mental illness rates are rising to unprecedented levels. Fortunately, wellbeing outcomes improve and increase as we move along the motivation continuum towards intrinsic motivation.

The next level of motivation is called *introjected* motivation. This is what our kids experience when they roll their eyes, exhale, and say, 'I should.' In adult terms, introjected motivation is the kind of motivation we show when, through gritted teeth, we refuse the chocolate cake and ice-cream because 'I really need to lay off the sugary treats.' We've absorbed the message that sugary treats are bad for us but we still want them. It's the 'have to' approach known as 'musturbation', as in 'I must do this' or 'I must do that'. Still a shallow form of motivation, introjected motivation is not particularly healthy or sustainable either. It's basically an internalised form of extrinsic motivation. It's just that we're punishing or rewarding ourselves on the inside.

An introjected form of motivation means the behaviour is being done because of what people will say, or because of how my parents will feel, or because otherwise I won't achieve my potential. Behaviour is contingent. The dynamic is 'I have to do this in order to feel good about myself and if I don't do this I won't feel good about myself.'

What a horrible place to leave our kids: where their worth is based on living up to our expectations, and they value themselves based on what we say about them. With introjected regulation, we think they're being compliant because they're great kids. We assume they're doing what we told them to in the absence of reward/punishment. But their behaviour is occurring because of fears of what happens when they fail to live up to our standards. Their self-worth is still being controlled, but with an internal voice.

Our child's motivation becomes more functional moving along the table to *identified* motivation. This is the kind of motivation we see in our children when they teach their siblings that 'It's better to share because that's how you be kind.' They're not in love with the idea. It's not a true reflection of who they are. But they're starting to become consciously aware that the behaviour they're focused on is a good idea. They've 'identified' that it's something to emulate.

Integrated motivation moves us into the deep end of the motivation continuum. This is the kind of motivation that says, 'I'm doing what's right because it feels right in my core.' Realistically, we probably won't see integrated motivation in our children until they're older. This is because that quality of integration requires a sense of identity. If our children don't know what their values are, because their sense of identity has not yet developed, they can't really behave in an integrated way. Therefore, this tends to show up once they know what they value and love it as a part of who they are.

And lastly, *intrinsic* motivation means doing an activity for the sake of the activity. Our child isn't cleaning their room because they'll be praised or given a treat, or to avoid something (which is external motivation). They're not doing it because they feel they should (which is introjected). They're not doing it because it's the right thing to do (which is identified). And they're not doing it because it's consistent with their values and having a clean room feels great (which is integrated). They're doing it because it's something they like to do for the activity itself … which raises an important question:

What child is intrinsically motivated to clean their room? In fact, what adult is?

Realistically, many tasks that our children are asked to do will never be intrinsically regulated. Do a quick audit. Tidying a bedroom? Probably externally motivated for most kids. Perhaps introjected as they get older. Potentially identified if cleanliness is an authentically prized value. For adults it could possibly reach to integrated motivational status if you truly enjoy the process of organising and tidying. But there's still an external motive: cleanliness.

How about exercise? For many kids, exercise is in the form of play. That is intrinsic. But once we parents get involved and start formalising and structuring their exercise, it easily slides back to the shallower motivational forms. Some children compete for awards and sponsorships, so that's extrinsic. Some exercise because they feel they need to stay in shape. That's introjected. Some exercise because they value health and want to be a healthy person – so we're shifting to identified. While unusual, the drive of a child who's in love with their sport or pastime *may* be integrated or intrinsically oriented. Adults, too, typically will exercise to stay in shape (introjected), because they recognise that health matters (identified) or because they value health and want to be around for the grandkids (integrated). Finding an activity or pastime that is done for the sake of the activity itself is true intrinsic motivation.

This motivation conversation is not a departure from our parenting discussion. It's the very heart of it. It's precisely why need-supportive parenting is so important for our children. Need-supportive parenting helps our children to operate in volitional, valued ways. It's somewhat important to use this approach to things like cleaning a room or brushing teeth. It becomes profoundly important to work with children in this way around issues such as standing up for a friend, making a safe and healthy choice at a party, studying for learning rather than grades, or participating fully in family and in life.

But when we create an environment that supports our children's three basic psychological needs, we move them towards deeper levels of motivation. When relationships are strong, when our children feel competent and capable, and when they sense autonomy in their decisions and activities, they lean away from external and introjected forms of motivation. They do things because they want to, because they feel right, and because they tap into their values and sense of self. Need-supportive parenting is what gets us there.

7

Need-supportive parenting

You will recall from Chapter 4 that I assessed several popularised and 'media-driven' parenting styles using the three concepts of *involvement*, *structure*, and *autonomy support*. What I didn't mention is that these three elements are the essentials of the parenting style that's at the heart of this book: need-supportive parenting.[1] *Involvement* builds relatedness, *structure* provides a serve of competence, and *autonomy support* meets a child's need for volition and choice.

When we – and in the context of this book, our children – experience these three basic psychological needs being satisfied, life will generally feel good and positive growth and development should follow. But equally, if we deprive our children of access to these basic needs of autonomy, competence, and relatedness, we increase the risk that they'll experience various forms of psychopathology.[2]

How to provide need support	What our child will experience
Be involved	A sense of relatedness
Provide structure	A sense of competence
Support their growth through safe, healthy decision making	A sense of autonomy

From time to time, the needs of relatedness, competence and autonomy can conflict. For example, parents can create tension between autonomy and relatedness needs. A child wants parental love *unconditionally*, so if the parent suggests, 'I'll love you more if you do that for me,' the child becomes confused. Two needs are being played off against each other in a mutually exclusive way. The parent is saying, 'You can have your autonomy or you can have my love (relatedness) but you can't have both.' This autonomy restrictive approach to meeting relatedness needs, which is known as *conditional parental regard*,[3] can potentially contribute to a range of psychological disturbances in a child.[4]

Similarly, perfectionism is experienced when a child experiences a battle between parental demands for competence and the parent makes relatedness (love) contingent on that high level of performance. Again, we see two needs being played off against each other in a mutually exclusive way. The child feels like he can only have his parent's love (relatedness) if he demonstrates an unattainable standard of competence. When competence (which is fragile) is not achieved, love is withdrawn, and anxiety, depression, and perfectionism result. (Extremes of tiger parenting are a case in point here.)

What is need-supportive parenting?

Need-supportive parenting is the kind of parenting that moves our children towards the deeper end of the motivation continuum. It's the kind of parenting that fosters understanding and internalisation. It's the kind of parenting that helps kids learn what's healthy, safe, and wise. It's the kind of parenting that facilitates children's internalisation of morality and values that will help them live better lives. And it does this, paradoxically, by reducing control and allowing our children's inherent goodness to be shaped and moulded as they develop and grow.

Unpacking need-supportive parenting

There's a formula or pattern we can follow to be need supportive in our parenting. We do it by:

1 encouraging choice and initiative by carefully guiding children through problem-solving and collaborative limit-setting,[5]

2 providing a clear rationale and explanation for behavioural requests when made, and

3 recognising the feelings and perspectives of the child.

Furthermore, need-supportive parents also minimise the use of controlling techniques as much as possible.

Sceptics might read that last sentence and suggest it sounds like permissive parenting, but this would be a mistake. Permissive parents possess an inability to set limits and/or make requests of their children. A need-supportive parent – far from being permissive – engages in the surprisingly challenging process of setting limits and working collaboratively on finding solutions to behaviour that's inconsistent with the reasonable things we ask of our kids. This isn't soft parenting. But neither is it harsh. Each chapter in Part 3 will provide examples of how to do this.

To put issues into perspective and properly foster your child's initiative requires a level of involvement and connection not seen in permissive styles of parenting. That doesn't mean need-supportive parents try to be their kids' best friends. Need-supportive parents encourage choice, but are not permissive. They consider their children's feelings, but they aren't pushovers.

Those characteristics of need-supportive parenting I outlined above might also seem like gentle parenting or free-range parenting. These styles do share some similarities with need-supportive parenting, but they lack the additional depth of involvement, structure, or autonomy support that need-supportive parenting requires.

In need-supportive parenting, the critical first point is where the real magic lies. It isn't rolling over and giving children all the power to go their own way and do their own thing. And it's not softly coddling the precious darlings while they have their 'feelings', which is a frequent criticism of any style of parenting that incorporates emotion coaching and awareness or consideration for a child's emotional world. Need-supportive parenting is a sophisticated and challenging process of *working with* children so they'll internalise and integrate safe, healthy, functional behaviours and be able to self-determine, rather than *doing things to* children to make them behave the way *we* want them to because they have to.

Here's a simple example. Your child tells you, 'I hate school. I don't want to go anymore.' Let's compare the major academic styles to see how they look in this example. I'll offer simple but generous interpretations of each to show them in their best light.

A lovingly engaged but permissive parent, low on demandingness but high on responsiveness, says, 'Oh sweetheart, school is so awful sometimes, isn't it? You know what? I love you and I want you to feel safe and comfortable. When you're ready to go to school, you come and let me know. If you want to stay home, that's fine. No pressure here.'

A lovingly engaged but authoritarian parent, high on demandingness but low on responsiveness, says, 'I'm sorry kiddo. You might not like it. It might feel horrible. But you know what? I love you and one day you'll thank me for prioritising your education above your feelings. If you don't go, we won't be able to do that special thing on the weekend we talked about. Now go and get ready to go to school because you really do need to be there and I expect that you *will* be there.'

A lovingly engaged authoritative parent, high on demandingness and high on responsiveness, says, 'I hear you. Going to school is one of those things you really hate to do. That's so hard, isn't it? But you know what? School's really important and even though you don't want to go, I'm going to insist that you get organised and go. And, if you can't do it, there will unfortunately be consequences.'

These are obviously simplified examples, but they convey the essential elements we have discussed already. They differ from an autonomy-supportive approach in important ways. Here's how an autonomy-supportive parent might respond:

'Let's explore what's going on … you really don't want to go to school today? Can you tell me more about that?'

[The parent listens to what the child has to say.]

'Well, now that we know you're not sick and you're just having a lousy day – and you don't like school much – let's talk about this some more and figure out why it's a problem.'

[After hearing them out in relation to their difficulties, they might explore further some of the reasons why school matters so much.]

'Where do we go from here? How can we problem-solve this together?'

Solutions could be as varied as both of your imaginations allow. The beauty of this process – and it is a *process* – is that a need-supportive approach (i) collaboratively seeks solutions that will work for everyone (ii) provides a clear rationale for the request, and (iii) considers the child's perspective. Because the child is responsible for determining a solution, their internal motivation to go in the direction that's been decided increases. It's not a parent determination. And therein lies the magic. Paradoxically, the more power we give to our children (with appropriate boundaries and context), the more they are open to our way of resolving challenges – but the less they need us to. When we invite them to find solutions, they become open to accepting our gentle guidance and supervision to keep them heading in safe, healthy, wise directions.

Where need-supportive parenting comes from

In the late 1970s, just a little over an hour to the southeast of Niagara Falls at the University of Rochester in upstate New York, two psychological scientists began a research programme that would change psychology forever. But they weren't parenting researchers. They were motivation researchers.

You have already met them: Professor Edward Deci and his collaborator, Richard Ryan, who went on to birth the Self-Determination theory that turned the science of motivation on its head. Their groundbreaking experiments have changed everything we once thought we knew about why people do what they do, including why children do what *they* do. As we learned in the last chapter, need support is at the heart of their work.

Ryan and Deci were publishing studies about how controlling environments affected adults. They were discovering that the more people felt that their choices were taken away, the less intrinsic motivation they had for doing pretty much anything. One of their Masters students, Wendy Grolnick, floated the idea of studying mothers and their babies. 'What happens,' she wondered, 'if we look at whether mothers are controlling or not when they interact with their children?' What happens when their needs are supported versus frustrated?' Will they be like the adults and lose motivation?

Her research question was given a green light and, in what has become a classic study by Wendy Grolnick, Ann Frodi, and Lisa Bridges, 41 mothers were observed in the psychology lab with their one-year-old children. Each mother was placed in a room with their child and given a toy, which they played with on the floor with their baby.[5] After a few minutes, the mother was given an intentionally ambiguous instruction: 'Sit next to your child while he (or she) plays with the toy.' The scene was videotaped for the following three minutes.

Pause and think about what you might do on the floor of a psychology lab, being videotaped and observed as you sit with your one-year-old and a toy – perhaps something like a shape-sorter. How are you going to engage? What do you want the experimenter to think of you? Of your baby? Will you sit passively and watch? Will you pick up the pieces and show your child where they go and how to push them into the appropriate holes? Or is there another way you'd respond?

As you might guess, the 41 mums reacted to the instruction in a variety of ways. Some proceeded to ensure that their child played 'the right way'. Whether they felt it was what was expected of them by the experimenter, or whether they felt pressure to impress and show the psychology researcher how advanced their child was, many mums spent the entire three minutes commanding their child to 'put the block in. No, not there. There!' The mums worked hard to help their babies learn how to do what the toy was designed for. They emphasised excellence, and success. Because the stakes felt high, they were anxious about how their child would do, and they behaved in controlling ways. The interactions with their children were full of correction and direction.

Other mothers took on the role of supporter rather than superintendent. Their approach was to give their child space to explore and problem-solve, and to assist if their child needed them.

Mums were rated on a continuum based on how controlling they were towards their child. A parent was highly controlling when they led the interaction, offered lots of correction and direction, and emphasised 'the right way' to play with the toy. Autonomy support was shown when mums followed their child's lead, offered gentle encouragement, and were attentive when the child felt stuck.

But the experiment wasn't quite over. The next part was crucial. It was about measuring the child's intrinsic motivation to play with an unfamiliar toy when mum wasn't involved. After the mother had been videotaped interacting with her child in the initial phase of the experiment, she was invited to sit off to the side. The child was given some other problem-solving toys to play with. Children of mums who were higher on the controlling side of the continuum tended to persist less with trying to play with these new toys. They demonstrated less interest in the tasks and gave up easily. It was almost as though they needed to have a guide beside them, showing them what to do, encouraging them with praise, and controlling their engagement with the task. Conversely, children of mums who were higher on the autonomy supportive side of the continuum were more inclined to play with the toys longer, find solutions, and explore the toys in novel ways.

Wendy Grolnick's study opened the door for dozens of subsequent studies investigating why children develop intrinsic motivation, persist when times are tough, and flourish in other aspects of their lives. For example, in 1993, Ed Deci and several colleagues ran a similar experiment to the one conducted by Grolnick, Frodi, and Bridges; only this time it was with children aged six or seven years old and their mothers.[6] In this study, the children of mothers who played with them in a more controlling way showed less motivation to play with those toys on their own compared with more need-supportive mother-child pairs, repeating what had been shown with the one-year-old children. These studies demonstrated a pattern for parents and children at all ages and stages: need support increases positive outcomes, while an environment that frustrates our children's needs reduces children's desires to be curious, persistent, and even compliant.

Let's revisit the needs and how we support them (from the start of this chapter) in light of these experiments: parents who were controlling (or autonomy restrictive) frustrated their children's *need* for autonomy. This, in turn, affected both the child's view of themself and their capability – because their mother didn't demonstrate belief in the child's ability to competently explore the task. That likely affected the relationship they felt with Mum. (We're talking small impacts here, but they compound over time.) All three needs are trampled when we fail to support children's autonomy.Mums who supported their children's autonomy needs gave them room to explore, but they also stayed involved and engaged. This made the kids feel connected, capable, and motivated.

We all have the very best of intentions for our children, but our effort to control our children's outcomes is the equivalent of trying to help a butterfly break its way out of a cocoon. Our 'help' – in the form of control, correction, and direction – risks rupturing the very development we're trying to encourage. The greater our anxiety about the outcomes our children achieve, the more controlling we will be as parents.[7]

There is a way for us to create a more need-supportive environment: trust that our children are intrinsically designed to grow and work things out. Chapter 10 will explore this in depth. For now, it's enough to recognise that the flow-on effect of our control and anxiety may be anxiety in our kids.

It's Getting Worse

Sadly, parents haven't got the memo: researchers are reporting parents becoming less supportive of their children's basic psychological needs in recent years. Specifically, parents are finding the urge to control their children irresistible.[8] Professor Stephan Collishaw, a University of Cardiff researcher specialising in psychological medicine and clinical neuroscience, told me that parents are 'becoming more autonomy restrictive over time, rather than more autonomy supportive'. He puts this down to something he observes anecdotally: 'Parenting – along with society as a whole – has become much more risk averse.' One way that this shows up 'is in the limits imposed on the autonomy of children.' His data shows we're literally going in the wrong direction in our parenting!

A summary of the science suggests that when we meet our children's basic psychological needs their brains work better, they're more intrinsically motivated to learn, persist, and be curious, and they do better at school.[9] Children are more excited to explore, create, and stick at something tough or tricky when we support their basic psychological needs.[10] Confidence and independence go up too. Restrictive and controlling parenting styles promote dependence on the parent (rather than independence) and undermine self-esteem.[11] Want your kids to score high on resilience and emotion regulation,[12] behave in prosocial ways, get better grades, and engage in less 'delinquent' behaviour?[13] Need-supportive parenting predicts these positive outcomes.

One final critical point on the value of need-supportive parenting. The IDeA centre (also known as the Individual

Development and Adaptive Education of Children at Risk Centre) is a research institution in Germany investigating new ways of making the world safer for our children. Dr Andreas Neubauer conducted a study of close to 1000 parents there during Covid-19 restrictions, attempting to understand how need-supportive parenting was related to both child *and* parent wellbeing. The parents had children who were developing typically, but there were also many neurodivergent children in the study. The average age of the youngest child in each family was nine years old. For three weeks, parents completed a diary questionnaire reporting on stress, family stability, child challenges, and parenting style. Neubauer found that need-supportive parenting was associated with happier kids, but also that the *parents* were doing better too. Need-supportive parenting isn't just good for kids. It's also great for parents.[14]

How does need-support parenting work?

I've pointed to a handful of studies to provide foundational evidence that need-supportive parenting – and specifically the autonomy-supportive element – elevates children's intrinsic motivation, academic outcomes, psychological adjustment, and wellbeing, plus their social and emotional development. But why is this so? Let's wrap up this chapter with the three key reasons autonomy-supportive parenting is so effective:

- First, it helps with children's need to feel connected and to belong. Children who feel that their parents see the world through their eyes, and whose parents encourage collaborative problem-solving, feel safe. They feel seen, heard, and valued. They feel secure in their warm and involved relationships. This is a powerful predictor of psychological adjustment, emotional and social development, wellbeing, and resilience.

- Second, it helps kids feel capable. Children who are given the opportunity to develop their own solutions to challenging situations know that their parents believe in them and *trust in their intrinsic capacity.* They feel competent. They know that they can navigate their environment (sometimes with their parents' support). This is a powerful predictor of intrinsic motivation, achievement, and wellbeing.

- Third, it gives children a sense that they're in control of their lives (with appropriate parental guidance where needed). That sense of control and volition is a powerful predictor of internalised morality, autonomous motivation, and wellbeing.

I'm not here to pretend this parenting style is simple. If you've spent a lifetime surrounded by intensive and controlling, behaviourally oriented parenting approaches like those outlined in previous chapters and popularised in the press, then need-supportive parenting may be the hardest parenting style you could try to adopt. It's hard to keep our child's frame of reference front and centre when they're being obstinate. It's hard to see the world through their eyes when it clashes so much with the way we see the world (through our own eyes).

In the next few chapters, we'll explore each of our children's basic psychological needs through the lenses of involvement, structure, and autonomy support.

8

The how-to's of healthy parental involvement

In this chapter, we poke and prod to really understand how to meet our children's relatedness needs. We'll examine what it is to be involved in our children's lives in healthy, functional, supportive ways and not in controlling and restrictive ways. But to understand why this matters, first we need to talk about rhesus monkeys in Wisconsin.

Psychologist Harry Harlow earned his PhD at Stanford University in 1930 by investigating the feeding behaviour of baby rats. After taking up a position at the University of Wisconsin (where the lab facilities didn't suit his work), Harlow moved forward with his research program by visiting the nearby zoo. His PhD student, a young man named Abraham Maslow,[1] was among those who helped Harlow observe primates in the zoo's enclosures. Out of this program, a stream of innovative research emerged about the primate's intelligence. Harlow and his students eventually put together a DIY zoo/lab back on campus, and this became his office for the next 40 years.

By the mid-1950s Harlow had become interested in rhesus monkeys and began breeding them. This wasn't typical – for psychologists or for Wisconsin! Researchers would typically import monkeys to their labs, but there were problems: the monkeys were difficult to obtain, they were often sick on arrival, and they rarely thrived. (The ethics of animal research was still a couple of decades away from being considered.)

When monkeys were born to unwell mothers, in an effort to keep the babies healthy, Harlow started to remove them from their mothers shortly after birth. He and his students fed the baby monkeys a formula they'd created. They developed a feeding pattern that seemed to sustain the monkeys, played with light/dark cycles, and adjusted temperatures until conditions were just right. Their monkeys were healthy and disease free. Success! But when Harlow introduced them into the company of the other monkeys, he discovered that the hand-reared ones were poorly adjusted. They lacked social skills. Monkeys raised in his nursery without their mother's involvement behaved in strange, often antisocial ways, compared with monkeys raised by their mothers. They weren't curious explorers who were socially engaged. Instead, they were shy, reclusive, even aggressive. And they were useless for experiments.

What happened next led to some of the most powerful discoveries in all of psychology. Harlow noticed that the monkeys reared in isolation were deeply attached to the cloth nappies he used for warmth or coverings in their cages. Was there something about the warmth? The fabric? The feel? Harlow designed some 'surrogate mothers', made of wire and wood. He also designed 'mothers' made of cloth. He placed one wire and one cloth 'mother' in each cage for each individual monkey. In some instances, he attached a bottle of milk to the wire and wood surrogate. In other cases, he added the milk bottle to the cloth surrogate. Then he watched. Would the monkeys prefer food? Or would they prefer warmth?

Harlow found that the monkeys overwhelmingly clung to the warmth of the cloth surrogate, regardless of where food and nourishment was.[2] They intrinsically craved touch with a warm, soft surrogate that was as close as possible to a real biological mother. They craved it so much that they'd cling to their cloth 'mother' while leaning across the cage, straining to reach the bottle attached to the wire 'mother' for food.

Recall from Chapter 1 that, around this time, academics like John B. Watson were saying children needed to be kept at arm's length. They weren't to be held or shown affection. These ideas had taken root in the mainstream of society, and psychologists and doctors were strongly anti-maternal (or anti anything that related to kindness, warmth, connection, and involvement). When the Grant Study was commencing, these austere child-rearing principles were still dominant. Harlow's research was conducted around the same time that the Grant study began. But Harlow's was not an 80-year process. Within a couple of years, he created a ripple that turned into a tsunami by showing a consistent need for parental involvement, affection, and warmth.[3]

Parental involvement creates more functional children

We're better parents when we're involved parents, as long as our involvement is need supportive rather than controlling. Our positive involvement in our children's lives makes our kids happier. For example, positive psychology researchers Kennon Sheldon, Todd Kashdan, and Mike Steger found that when parents are responsive to and involved with their children, their children's vagal tone increases.[4] Having higher vagal tone means that your child's body can relax faster after stress. This is good!

Sheldon and his colleagues discovered that when parents are involved in their kids' lives, those children experience lower levels of psychological pain and their happiness is enhanced.[5] You know this from all of those experiences where your child has been hurt, physically or emotionally, and you've been there for them with a hug and a kiss – and no lecture. Your child calmed down faster, felt safer, and got back into life more quickly than they might have if they'd had to tackle this experience on their own. This is, in part, because your involvement increased vagal tone, helping to soothe her.

In another experiment, Randal Day and Laura Padilla-Walker, two psychology researchers at Brigham Young University, found that when dads of young adolescents were involved in their children's lives, and those children consequently sensed connection in their relationship, the kids were less likely to experience depression, anxiety, and other internalising disorders. They were also less likely to behave in antisocial ways, with anger, rebellion, or destructive actions. Also, when mothers were involved and connected with their children, Day and Walker found children were more prosocial (kind, considerate ... just nice) and more hopeful about the future.[6] This is a list of so many things you might want to see on your child's developmental journey. It's a sign that things are going well.

In their acclaimed book, *The Irreducible Needs of Children: What Every Child Must Have to Grow, Learn, and Flourish,* Stanley Greenspan and T. Berry Brazelton describe 'the need for ongoing, nurturing relationships' as the first and primary need of our children. Clark University professor Wendy Grolnick states emphatically, 'If I had to choose between involvement, structure, and autonomy support, I'd choose involvement so long as the involvement is offered in a need-supportive way. It's *that* important.'[7]

What involvement looks like

The etymology of involvement is Latin (*involvere*), and it means to envelop, surround, or literally to 'roll into'. Involvement is showing love, warmth, and affection. In a practical sense, involvement can be ferrying children from one activity to another or eating together; bathing a young child or having bedtime stories. It's being across their academic, sport, or cultural experiences. How are they going at school or on their sports team? Are they aware that you care, and that you're there to support them if they need you? At a deeper level, involvement is being present in their spaces, their conversations, and their activities: Their world. This involvement can often be (and probably should most often be) benign background involvement. Perhaps you're in the kitchen while they're in the living room or the back yard. But you're involved and aware. You're having regular conversations to know about their daily discoveries, their friendships, and their life.

It's also *their* involvement in *your* world. Are they cleaning their room *with* you, or peeling vegetables for dinner *with* you? Are they involved in dinnertime conversations with you, playing music with you, learning a new game with you, and exercising with you? Our children want to be in our world, particularly when they're young. Are your little ones – and your big ones – welcome at the dinner table while you're chatting with friends after a barbecue? Do they get to be involved in your work, your hobbies, and even your chores?

The costs of controlling involvement

At the conclusion of a parenting presentation on a cold Canberra night, a father approached me. 'I used to have a great connection with my son,' he explained, 'but we don't talk anymore. I don't get him. I don't know what happened, but something's changed since he turned 12. He's angry. He's disrespectful. I feel like I've lost my little buddy.'

We chatted briefly about adolescent development and his son's broader situation, including his friendships, schooling, extracurricular interests, sleep, screens, and more. Everything seemed to be okay, and so I shifted gear. 'Tell me about how much correction and direction your son hears from you.' The man described their interactions. He had high expectations of his son. He pushed him to do well, put in more effort, be better.

This dad was clearly involved in his son's life with genuine intentions. But involvement can take many forms. Some forms of involvement are helpful. Helpful involvement is when a child feels connected and so his relatedness need is supported and satisfied. Unhelpful involvement is when a child feels controlled. In this case, a child's relatedness need will feel frustrated. The involvement is there, but control can undermine connection, and so the quality of the relationship is hollow.

I asked this dad what the ratio was in their relationship between correction and direction versus *connection*. Then, a humble confession: 'We don't connect like we used to.' He confirmed that most of his interactions were 'bossing my boy around'.

Continuing, he described their history of fun times wrestling on the floor, kicking a ball, or engaging in idle chit-chat. But that was when his son was younger. Straightaway, this man could see that his correction and direction left his son feeling unseen, unheard, and devalued, like a chattel or possession. It was interfering with his son's need for relatedness. The advice may have been 'involvement', but because his son perceived it as controlling, it was creating a wedge in their relationship, and in his son's wellbeing.

If we step back and consider the son's frame of reference, he probably felt like 'Dad's always on my back about my grades and my room and my friends and my music … and everything.' As our conversation wound up, I saw resolution (and perhaps revolution) in a dad committed to spend more time connecting, with less control, starting with a bike ride the next day, and a quick camping trip to the coast within the month. Let's acknowledge that our children do need correction and direction. There should be reasonable expectations and behavioural standards. But how we have those conversations matters tremendously. We'll explore this theme throughout the remainder of the book.

Healthy vs unhealthy involvement

According to Professor Wendy Grolnick, involved parents do three things:

1 invest time, attention, and energy

2 gain knowledge about their children's lives, and

3 provide support.

As the dad I spoke with in Canberra discovered, we can do this in a controlling way, or we can do it in a need-supportive way. Investing time, attention, and energy into our child's school experience can be helpful or harmful. It depends on *how* we do it. When we invest time and attention in a controlling way, we pore over our children's results, push our child to do better, corral them into extracurricular coaching, and harangue them for failing to win the dux of kindergarten award! It's that whole 'parent harder' kind of approach to involvement. The investment, the knowledge, and the support are set up with the best of intentions. But it's us setting the expected standard for them and pushing (sorry … supporting) them to achieve it because we have unilaterally determined that it matters. There's that intense and controlling involvement that undermines individual motivation and wellbeing. The involvement we share is targeted towards other ends rather than being an end in itself.

A form of involvement in schoolwork that supports relatedness needs looks more like us taking an interest, asking how they're doing, and inviting them to think about how they'd like to do at school, *and why*. And it's based on developmentally appropriate timing. Our six-year-old doesn't need to be chasing straight As! It's not important for our Grade 3 child to be reading at a high-school level! But … if they love reading and happen to be doing well, great; because they're volitionally seeking it. Perhaps they're doing it for the sake of the activity itself. It lights them up. Learning is intrinsically motivating! Our support and involvement will facilitate rather than undermine that motivation.

Recall the Grolnick study of mothers with their one-year-old children? Mothers were involved in their children's play in different ways. Some were controlling, trying to help their child play 'the right way'. Others were supportive, exploring together and allowing their child to experience the natural delight that comes through their own discovery. Involvement that supports relatedness needs creates connection; that sense of being seen, heard, and valued. Involvement that is controlling disrupts the experience of connection and relatedness.

Healthy need-supportive involvement requires effort. We have to break away from the inertia of our screens, the couch, or our agendas. We also have to break away from the inertia of our upbringing, our insecurity, our ego, and our desires for our children to fulfil their potential based on our preferences.

'They're only doing it for attention!'

It's pretty easy to sit here and read a book that tells you to be warm and loving and involved. It all makes sense. Research and experience tell us it matters. We nod along to chapters like this easily. Reading about things that resonate is friction free.

But when it's 7.50 am and our child is refusing to go to school, creating a need-supportive environment that builds a sense of relatedness and connection is usually the last thing on our mind. How are we supposed to do this 'relatedness' support when our nerves are frayed, and we're ready to crack? Instead of need support, we're tag-teaming our partner so we can wrestle arms into uniforms, feet into socks, and bags onto shoulders to get our child out the door, into the car, and off to school. That feels like a pretty controlling form of involvement, and definitely not supportive of relatedness needs.

So what are the options?

1 Get mad and force a child to comply, carrying them to the car in their pyjamas if necessary?

2 Let the child be and refuse to engage until the child is calm and rational (which can be leveraged into the ultimate procrastination tool by a child)?

3 Impose sanctions on a wilful or challenging child, sending them to their room, threatening to remove privileges, or even hitting them? (Surveys indicate a surprising level of endorsement for smacking a child in Australia, the USA, England, New Zealand, and Canada.)

While none of these is ideal (and we've probably tried them all!), perhaps the most common parenting trope – all too often promoted by behavioural scientists and old-school parents for many decades –

is believing that when our children are behaving in a challenging way, 'They're just doing it for attention.' The thinking is that if you give a child attention after they've behaved poorly, you'll reinforce their poor behaviour. If you 'reward' their poor behaviour with your attention, every time your child wants something, they'll play up. Therefore, the best thing we can do – according to this behaviourist mindset – is to sever our connection with them when they behave in challenging ways.

Sadly, this approach is pervasive, particularly for parents of children with additional needs. Kids on the spectrum or who are diagnosed with ADHD are often accused of 'attention-seeking behaviour'. Parents are routinely advised to ignore their child when they behave 'that way'. This attitude is an unhelpful relic.

Perhaps we might do better if we recognise that a child may be acting this way because:

- They feel disconnected (so it's not attention-seeking, but relatedness-seeking)

- They feel incompetent or incapable (so it's not attention-seeking, but structure- or support-seeking)

- They feel like they have no autonomy (so it's not attention-seeking, but autonomy-seeking)

Children behave in challenging ways when the environment is frustrating their basic psychological needs. The idea that our child is attention-seeking and ought to be ignored until they behave in a more 'appropriate' manner is unfair, unscientific, and lacking compassion. Today's best science comprehensively rejects this approach. We now know that children are seeking attention (which is really involvement) because they *need* it in order to be healthy and happy. And paradoxically, giving them attention through our involvement when they're being challenging will reduce their difficult behaviour in the moment, and over the longer term as well, because that gentle, kind attention will help them regulate, feel safe, and think clearly. It builds a sense of security and safety. It promotes trust and predictability.

Cutting involvement and disconnecting from your child only reinforces their feelings of unworthiness and incompetence, and creates a bigger relationship divide, which exacerbates problematic behaviour because their environment frustrates their needs even more.

What it all boils down to is straightforward.

If your child is seeking attention, give it to them! Involve yourself. Create the connection they need. It's less that you're dealing with a challenging child, and more that you're helping your child deal with a challenge. This re-frame is important.

How ignoring your child affects connection

Let's step this out by considering your child's experience. It's been a rough day. They're emotionally out of sorts. They haven't eaten enough, they're tired, and you've just told them that their plans for the night are not in line with what's actually going to happen. This stuff happens to kids *every* day! How do they feel? Probably disgruntled and agitated. Their emotions begin to spill over a little.

The frustration starts seeping out of their eyes in the form of tears. If we're having one of our lesser moments, perhaps we walk over to them and say:

> 'Quit crying or I'll give you something to cry about.'
> 'If you keep that up, I'm not even going to talk to you.'
> 'Don't worry about it. You'll be fine. It's not that big a deal.'

Or perhaps you look at your partner and say, 'She gets like this all the time. I'm sure she only does it so I'll give her attention or cave in and give her what she wants.'

Let's pause and ask what 'lessons' your child is learning in this situation. My guess?

Through an unwillingness to be involved in a need-supportive way, your child is learning that her parents lack kindness, perspective, and compassion; that she can't trust us with the tender feelings of her heart, which means that vulnerability is not an option in your relationship. She doesn't feel that you're willing to act in her best interest. Your child learns that emotions get her into trouble, so she should bury them in future. And she figures that her needs are secondary to those of everyone around her. The list goes on, although there is one more that needs special emphasis:

Your child will internalise the belief that she doesn't matter; she is not valuable as a person; she is not worthy.

And her relatedness need will be crushed.

Hard to read? I hope so. Viewing the world through our children's eyes is an essential skill of need-supportive parents.

Simply knowing this, I'd imagine, provides opportunity for some regret. It's not possible to be a parent without failing – often – in one of the ways I've just described. But this isn't about parent-shaming. This is not about judgment. According to Daniel H. Pink in his book, *The Power of Regret,* 'Regret makes us human' and 'regret makes us better.' In fact, 'its very purpose is to make us feel worse, because by making us feel worse today, regret helps us do better tomorrow.'

When our child is driving us to breaking point, it's more important than ever that the environment supports their relatedness needs. They need to feel safe. They need to trust us. Then they can regulate their emotions and work through their challenges. Again, for emphasis: connection is feeling seen, heard, and valued. And it comes from someone taking the time to be involved in a supportive (but not controlling) way. Where there is supportive involvement, there is the feeling of connection. And with connection, there is life in a relationship.

In contrast to the less connected responses I shared on the last page, how would your child feel if you involved yourself in a supportive way, by saying something like: 'It seems like your day's been pretty rough. Do you need a hug? Would you like some space right now? How can I help?' Chances are that your child would melt into your arms, because they would feel seen, heard, and valued. The relationship has life.

To understand what's in the hearts of our children, we must listen. And to truly listen, we must be involved; it requires taking time. We don't build relationships by watching the clock. Relationships don't work on principles of efficiency. Evidence from around the world consistently shows that our children thrive and our relationships flourish when we invest ourselves through healthy and supportive forms of involvement. Time in the morning. Time in the afternoon and evening. Time in the car, in the kitchen, in the tiny micro-moments of time confetti where we could stare at our phone or do something productive but instead we pause and give time to our child. Time at lights-out. Time on weekends. Time during holidays. One of the greatest gifts you can give those you love is time. Love, to a child, is spelled T-I-M-E.

Some simple involvement ideas

Let's get practical. The ideas below might sound obvious, but they are profoundly effective in supporting your child's relatedness needs – and they're often things we know we ought to do but struggle to actually do.

Take every opportunity

Sometimes our children speak to us at inconvenient moments. Other times the things they speak to us about feel mundane and boring. Our response may be to sigh, stare at our device, and humour them. Instead, see their desire to talk with you as an opportunity to meet the need they have to feel a sense of relationship; an opportunity to understand what's inside your child, making them tick, inspiring them, and igniting them. Any time they talk to you, they're opening their life up and inviting you in. What a privilege! When they talk with you, recognise that they could as easily be staring at a screen. Instead, they've chosen you. Grab the opportunity with both hands and devour it. And if you really can't, explain why and tell them when you can be involved.

Be where your feet are

Ever had one of those conversations where your child is talking, they're looking at you and you're nodding, but you know you're not actually listening? The lights are on but no one's home. You're thinking about something else. They ask you a question and you stammer as you try to answer, clueless about what they were saying. Chances are, you repeat their last four words because that's all you heard. And you say, 'I was listening. I was just thinking about ...'

Being where your feet are is simple. It means you situate your brain in the same place your feet are placed. If your feet are in the kitchen in front of your 5-year-old, you put your brain there too, rather than on the day's four phone calls and 63 emails, or the pickups and dropoffs for your other children that afternoon. If your feet are under the covers in bed, next to those of your spouse or partner, you put your brain in bed next to your spouse or partner too. When you are where your feet are, you'll be involved. And when you're involved, your child will feel connected; related.

Smile

A smile is the key to the lock of your child's heart. If you feel glad to be involved with your child, remember to let your face know.

Smile. It makes your child feel welcome and wanted. And it invites warmth and conversation.

Devices down

Enough said.

Create opportunities for unusual discussions

Hypotheticals requiring short answers are terrific conversation starters that make involvement fun. 'If you could ...?' and 'Would you rather ...?' questions are easy and lighthearted. Here are a few tried and tested conversations you might have:

- You find a book and begin to read, only to discover that *it is your life*. You get to the point you're at now: do you turn the page, knowing you'll be unable to change the events to come?

- If you had to choose, would you rather get uglier or dumber? (Or reverse it: would you rather get more attractive or smarter?)

- What would you do if you discovered you only had 24 hours to live?

- If Jurassic Park were real, would you visit?

- If you could spend the day in a great library studying anything you wanted, what would you study?

- If you could ask your future self from the year 2050 one question, what would you want to know?

- If you could spend an hour with anyone who ever lived, who would it be? Why? What would you ask?

- If your stuffed animals could talk, what would they say?

- If you had to be stuck in a TV show for a month, which show would you choose? What character would you be?

- If you could be one age forever, what age would you choose?

- If you were torturing someone with music, what's the one song you'd choose to play on repeat?

- If you found a talking wild animal and could ask it a question, what would you ask?

Sometimes the best conversations come out of stories from your own life. When did you do something dumb, say something embarrassing, or make everyone laugh? Better yet, when did your children? You can ask questions that are about real situations (sneaking cookies, breaking a picture or window with a ball, 'borrowing' the car at 10 o'clock at night).

The idea is to be creative and playful.

Show interest

I know that sometimes conversations with our children are a bit of a slog. Discussions about dinosaurs and dragons can be draining after a while. And when kids are upset about a schoolyard skirmish or a social media squabble, while we care, we all have those moments where it can feel tedious going through it with them. But ask questions. 'How did you feel?' 'What options do you have?' 'How can I help?'

Get curious, not furious

When your child says something you find annoying, perplexing, or outrageous, focus on understanding, not reprimanding. That means explore rather than explode. Ask questions. Slow things down. A useful script might be, 'Wow, that wasn't what I expected. Why do you feel like that, I wonder?' Curiosity creates connection.

Plan activities to do together

These could include water play or ground play with little kids. It might be baking or drawing with bigger kids. Or maybe you can play games, arrange an outing, or do something physically active together.

Create routines that encourage involvement and connection

This could include having meals together, enjoying planned and intentional conversations at the dinner table about 'grateful things', having a weekly family games night, having a once-a-month conversation about big topics, reading together at bedtime, or having a special outing for breakfast with one parent while the other parent gets to sleep in or relax.

Some more principles to practise

Review the way you use your time

We're surrounded by ways to distract ourselves: online streaming platforms, social media, excessive work, to name a few. Constantly pouring time into these things – on a solo basis – is a recipe for lousy relationships. People with extraordinary relationships enjoy downtime, but they also leverage opportunities to be involved, intentional, and connected.

Build your catalogue of connection experiences, not your catalogue of movies to watch on a streaming service with your earpods in. Break through the inertia of the screen, make the effort, and reap the benefits of being involved and creating the connection. Be honest about what you do with your time and find ways to maximise your time 'in' with your kids by really being present.

Allow your worlds to cross over

Our children want to be in our world. Much of the time they're fascinated by the work we do. We have a tendency, however, to brush them aside. It might be for their safety. More often, however, it's due to efficiency. We want to cook dinner, clean up, or do our tasks without having to slow to a child's pace. You might be surprised by the benefits of bringing your children into your world. Let them try what you're doing. Savour their involvement and help them feel connected. When they make a mistake with the cheese grater or milk carton and mess goes everywhere, take a breath, smile, and let them help you with the clean-up. No tears. No fuss. Just loving involvement. They'll learn, and they'll love being there with you.

Take the ride, not the wheel

When a child begins to talk with us, it's tempting to take over the conversation. We hear about an experience from their day and we want to share a similar experience from our own lives. We listen to a challenge they face and hope to share how we overcame one just like it. The temptation is to become prematurely autobiographical ('I remember when that happened to me'), comparing ('That's not as bad as what I faced'), or even reassuring ('I'm sure you'll be fine'). We feel good when we fix everything. But this is taking over.

Instead, let your child stay behind the wheel and steer. You go along for the ride, listen closely, and see where you end up. Chances are that your child will sense your trust, feel empowered, and work things out for themselves.

Honour the relationship

When we honour our children we look past petty grievances, weaknesses, and mistakes, and we affirm the intrinsic wonder and beauty inside them. We honour our children by:

- offering acceptance (especially when we want to disagree or be petty)

- considering their perspective (even when we want to have our own way)

- highlighting their significance in our lives

- recognising and reminding ourselves of their positive qualities

- showing love by doing things with them

- making amends when we get it wrong, even if it's just a little thing

- being responsive to their feelings and honouring them in those feelings.

Remember the three most important words

Unconditional love is a potent force for creating safety, security, and resilience. It's important to communicate to our children that we love them, and one way is verbally. The security children derive from hearing this from you matters. Some cultures – some families – shy away from overt expressions of love and appreciation. This idea can be tricky. If you have it in you, however, it's powerful to say 'I love you' often to your children. (Of course, your involvement with them must be consistent with those words.)

But they're not the most important words a child can hear, nor are they the words that will demonstrate unconditionality. The three most important words are the ones that come after 'I love you.' They are 'no matter what'.

The true meaning of involvement

It's easy to be involved in our child's world in controlling ways. Involvement can be pushing them to do their homework, practise harder, play sport with more passion, do more, be more, achieve more. We can up the involvement by monitoring their online worlds or checking on their friendships (or merely by hassling them to get their bedrooms tidy). This kind of involvement is autonomy restrictive. It fails to satisfy our children's relatedness needs because our involvement doesn't help them feel connection: seen, heard, and valued.

Though they may not show it, our children are desperate to enter our world and connect with us. Even more, they crave the opportunity to bring us into their world and share their experience of life with us (yes, even when they grunt in response to our query about how their day was). We often get caught up in planning the perfect party, the heavenly holiday, or the exciting event where we can all connect and make memories. This can be a useful strategy, but a focus on consistent small episodes of involvement and connection will do more for happiness, wellbeing, and growth than the occasional big thing. Simply do what's important but unspectacular, over and over again.

Involvement, connection, warmth, responsiveness … this relatedness need is known by and supported by so many ideas with so many names, but the one thing I've rarely seen it called in parenting science is the one thing we most need to call it: love. It's love – or loving connection – that draws our children to us, because it's the truest way they can feel seen, heard, and valued. It's love that gives life. It's love that comes from involvement, creates connection, and satisfies the relatedness need better than any other form of relationship.

How to create structure that supports a child

In her bestselling book on cross-cultural childrearing, *Hunt, Gather, Parent,* Michaeleen Doucleff visits a village in Mexico's Yucatán Peninsula, interviewing mothers about traditional parenting practices. Doucleff is immediately struck by how helpful the children are, and how willingly they involve themselves in contributing around the house. One mother, Maria, describes to Doucleff how 5-year-old Alexa always wants to join her as she prepares tortillas. Alexa's involvement typically generates a lot of mess. Because Alexa is so young (and tortilla-making is a relatively advanced skill) she does a generally terrible job of making the tortillas. Her tortillas are neither big, nor round, nor flat. Instead, they're small, misshapen, and lumpy; not a good combination for a tortilla lover. Her fingers lack the dexterity to manipulate and manoeuvre the tortillas. Her forearms and wrists lack the strength to press and flatten them. Alexa lacks skill and knowledge. Tortilla-making is beyond her developmental capacity.

Doucleff finds this situation provocative. She reminds Maria that young children tend to make things harder, not easier. She also acknowledges her own tendency to discourage her young daughter,

Rosy, from being involved in any tasks at all. The inefficiency and additional burden of juggling the task and the child are too much. Doucleff is inclined to fix things. Fast. And then exclude her daughter from helping in future! Why does Maria let Alexa make a mess? And why doesn't she teach her how to make tortillas properly?

As Doucleff describes in *Hunt, Gather, Parent*, Maria does not correct her daughter. She doesn't point out the mistakes, lumps, inconsistencies, or other elements that make the tortilla inedible. She makes no attempt to offer 'constructive criticism', guide her daughter to a higher level of tortilla-making capability, or otherwise make sure she's doing it right. She doesn't even scold her for making a mess or require that Alexa tidy everything up. To the contrary, Maria understands that this tortilla-making business is complex and a five-year-old, no matter how hard she tries, isn't going to get it right. Maria invites her daughter's involvement and encourages her to try it out until she's had enough. Tortilla-making proficiency will take years to develop, and from Maria's point of view, that's fine. There is no rush.

The crux of the exchange occurs when Maria tells Doucleff that she lets her little girl join in even if she makes a giant mess because 'that is the way to teach children'.

I take two lessons from this story. The first concerns what we discussed in the previous chapter: involvement. In bringing Alexa close, Maria teaches a simple but deep lesson about worthiness, belonging, and feeling cared for. It's a perfect case study of involvement and supporting our children's relatedness needs.

The second lesson is about how we can support our children's competence needs. Recall that competence is developing a sense of mastery or capability, and our children crave the opportunity to develop this capacity. The desire to get better at things is innate. In her conversation with Doucleff, Maria stressed that whether her daughter's involvement was useful or not was irrelevant. Alexa wanted to help and so Maria let her help. In addition to meeting Alexa's relatedness need, she allowed her the opportunity to experiment, play, and build skills. Maria seemed to intuitively understand the motivation continuum: if she focuses on rewards (including praise) or punishments (including criticism or correction), Alexa will only make tortillas when something is in it for her or when she knows she won't get into trouble for getting things wrong. Instead, Maria intentionally allows her daughter to work alongside her, making mistakes: Maria knows that, as a mother, she's playing a long game. As long as Alexa is intrinsically motivated to work on tortillas with her mum, her skill improves. The enticement of developing a skill and staying close to Mum is all the motivation that's needed. She's swimming in the deep end of the motivation pool. This behaviour is becoming internalised: it's intrinsically motivating because it builds relationship and capability. In time, she'll make pro-level tortillas. Competence achieved.

Inspired by Maria's example, I decided to try a similar approach with some chores on a quiet Saturday afternoon. Some trees in our yard had dropped leaves all over the perimeter of my freshly trimmed lawn. As I walked into the yard I called to my two youngest daughters, inviting them to help me pick up the leaves. My 12-year-old rolled her eyes but reluctantly followed me. My 8-year-old yelled in frustration, 'I hate picking up leaves!' This seemed funny to me, because I couldn't think of a time she'd *ever* helped with any form of yard work. How would she know she hates it? Rather than being forceful, I smiled and said, 'It would be great to spend some time with you while we pick up the leaves.' No more than two minutes later, both of my daughters were alongside me, clearing the mess from the yard. An invitation to be involved and together was, inexplicably, too good to pass up. Score one for *involvement*.

Some of the leaves were a little out of reach. I retrieved a rake from the shed, returning moments later. I had only used the rake for three seconds when my 8-year-old asked if she could do the raking. Delighted at this suddenly willing helper, I showed her how to reach the leaves at the back of the garden and pull them forward without destroying plants or removing layers of topsoil. Channelling my inner Yucatán mother, I handed her the rake, cringing inwardly as she jabbed it through greenery and reefed piles of soil out of the garden and onto the lawn. But I held strong. I said nothing. And I watched in awe as she gardened for close to 30 minutes without complaint, even after I had finished the work I planned to do. (Her 12-year-old sister hung around for the duration as well.) The mess? It wasn't so bad. Ten extra minutes of clearing up (later that day when she wasn't watching) and everything was neat and tidy again.

Contrast this approach to the way we might typically respond to our children's efforts to help, or the way they complete mandatory jobs. When a child messes up, our instinct is to dive in and offer correction. Our intentions are good. But unless there's risk of harm, our instincts may also be misplaced and unhelpful. They undermine our children's sense of competence.

Does this mean we should accept mediocrity? In short, the answer is no. But there's an autonomy-supportive way to teach this, which I'll get to later in the chapter.

Let's look deeper into the basic psychological need of competence. What is it? How does it work? What do we need to do to create an environment that supports competence? How do we help our children improve? In this chapter we'll discuss the important role of *structure* and how high-quality parents provide structure to guide and support their children.

Competence

Competence is the sense that we're mastering our environment. It's that feeling of being capable, on top of things. We know how to operate in a particular setting, and we do it satisfactorily. Adults and children; we're wired to seek competence.

In a supportive environment where relatedness and autonomy needs are being met, a child will try to be competent at *everything*! As a parent, you'll have heard your toddler or preschooler demanding, 'Let me do it.' Little children want to experience and master every task. The world is full of exciting opportunities to figure things out, and they want to go for it. Your big kids will be the same: 'I'm fine Mum. I can do it on my own.'

We can tell we're creating an environment that supports competence in our children when they show two things: curiosity and creativity. Curiosity demonstrates a fascination with the environment and how things work. Curious kids have a penchant for seeking new experiences, knowledge, and feedback. They're absorbing information and adjusting their behaviour accordingly, mastering their environment along the way. Curious kids are sending a signal that their environment is supportive and they're becoming competent.

Creativity provides that same signal. When a child is organising or inventing, they're developing and demonstrating competence and capability.

And these two characteristics of competence development show up best during an activity that children are potentially experiencing less and less, yet needing more and more: play. That's what was really happening when Alexa made tortillas with Maria. And it's what my daughter was doing with the rake in the yard. Competence develops in a variety of ways, but few are as powerful and effective as play.

Structure

A scan through the history books shows that parents have long been encouraged to raise well-socialised, capable children. Once scientists involved themselves, the pathway was thought to be based on responsiveness (love) and demandingness (limits). But in high-quality parenting that supports children's needs, when we talk about structure, it's not the same as the concept of *demandingness* in this traditional paradigm.

Structure refers to boundaries, expectations, and limits. The purpose of structure is to show children what's expected so that life feels predictable, and so everyone can work together to make things happen when and how they should. Creating structure helps our children understand how their behaviour relates to their outcomes. We have structure so our children's environment makes sense. By comparison, unpredictability creates confusion, ineffectiveness, maladaptivity, a loss of self-efficacy, and even dysfunction. Structure removes those negatives and provides a pathway forward. It's a little opaque, but it will make more sense if we understand structure in need-supportive terms.

Structure is basically about *scaffolding*. We use scaffolding around buildings to provide access to unreachable places for workers. It makes an impossible task (like reach high places) achievable. In parenting, scaffolding involves requests and prompts, boundaries and limits. It's what we provide so that our children can feel and experience competence, and develop capabilities they don't yet have.

I'll offer two brief analogies. First, think of structure like the string on a kite. The kite can only fly if there's a string being held by someone on the ground. If you throw a kite into the air without the string, it falls back to the Earth. The same thing happens to children when there's no structure, no expectation, no socialisation process. The string (which is our structures and limits) provides tension. It holds the kite (the child) steady. The wind now rushes over the wings of the kite and, because the string holds it in place, allows it to lift. Our children need that string (the structures, limits, and boundaries) so they can receive the lift they need to fly. Without the string, they'll never reach the heights offered by the structures the string provides.

Analogy two: a soccer game. The structure of the game is that there are two teams, a goal, boundaries for the field, and structural elements (rules), like the need to remain 'onside', not using hands, and so on. This structure allows the game to be played in a predictable and enjoyable way that works, and that newcomers can join in with.

Structures can include routines for the morning, and time-targets such as an 8 pm bedtime. School five days per week is an example of structure. Swimming lessons every Tuesday at 4.30 pm is an example of structure. But while these are demonstrations of structure, structure isn't limited to rigid, time-stamped appointments in the diary. Structure includes flexible but regular ways of living a healthy life. A bedtime routine that includes brushing teeth and hair, singing songs, reading a story, and meditating or saying a night-time prayer – these are examples of structure. But so too is knowing that certain tasks must be completed before screens and gaming or social media are allowed. Structure exists in social contexts as well. Structure is understanding that hitting siblings is not okay and will lead to outcomes that a child may prefer to avoid.

Structure and autonomy support

Recall from Chapter 8 that controlling forms of involvement from parents are unhelpful, but autonomy-supportive involvement is profoundly useful. One of the main areas of parental involvement is schooling. Studies show that the degree to which parental involvement in schooling is autonomy supportive reliably predicts how the child will feel about schoolwork, and can influence how they do at school. When kids feel volitional about their school involvement and their academic goals and outcomes, they feel more positively towards school than those who experience autonomy restrictive forms of involvement where participation, choices and even goals are controlled by parental demand and expectation. These findings underscore that the controlling approach keeps us at the shallow end of the motivation continuum, where motivation is external. Autonomy support, however, creates buy-in. With autonomy-supportive involvement we are in the deep end of the motivation continuum, and motivation is intrinsic.

This principle of supporting autonomy is not just relevant to *involvement*, nor does it only apply to the school context. Supporting autonomy overlaps with developing and implementing structure as well. It's not just that we *have* structure that matters. It's how we create and implement the structure that is key.

Establishing structures in a controlling/autonomy-restrictive way predicts extrinsic motivations and less optimal outcomes. We see this happen when we lay out the rules autocratically. Maybe you've had this experience? You walk into the room and tell the kids exactly how it's going to be from now on. Everyone *is* going to be kind. Everyone *is* going to help with the cleaning and other chores. Everyone *is* going to bed on time. And for about 15 minutes everyone does exactly what you have said they should do because they're so afraid. But the buy-in drops off. The fear fades. In a short time it's like you never had the conversation in the first place. Those structures you outlined? They're gone.

Maybe you've also had the alternative experience, where you've been autonomy supportive when establishing structure, rules, and expectations, rather than autonomy restrictive? Instead of laying down the law, you've sat with your children and described what you're struggling with. You've sought their input. You've invited their ideas. You've talked through the challenges that need to be overcome and asked them how the day (or your family life) might be better structured to work through those difficulties. Chances are, those structures stuck. The kids bought-in, helped out, and improved things for everyone. It may even have been longer lasting than the Captain Cranky move you pulled in the controlling scenario. Why? It's autonomy-supportive structure that predicts more internalised motivations and optimal outcomes.

Take some examples of school and extracurricular activities, duties and chores, or getting along with siblings – each of these requires some kind of structure. We can demand that our children do as they're told. Or we can work together to discover solutions and structures in an autonomy-supportive way. The collaborative approach to structure helps our children feel good about the rules, while still giving parents capacity to offer counsel, direction, and experience if required. We can choose control. Or we can choose to support autonomy as we create structures that facilitate life flow.

Structure = problem solving

Where controlling structure is a form of unilateral and autocratic decision-making by parents, autonomy-supportive structure is a process of collaborative problem-solving with children. While developing structure in an autonomy-supportive way is preferable, please don't take that to mean we are putting children in charge. *Children don't make the rules.* This is *not* a permissive process where we let children take control and act entirely independently. Rather, parents develop structures – or patterns and processes for working through challenges – collaboratively with their children, but those structures must be consistent with the wisdom and experience our years of life advise. We have an obligation – a parental duty – to be guides for our children, and to develop structures with them for their benefit. If children can develop appropriate structures and rules without our involvement, that's great! But we have an obligation to be involved in the process to be sure things are headed in a safe direction. Occasionally parents mistakenly think that autonomy-supportive approaches mean we hand the wheel over to the children and let them steer. While that is the ultimate goal, it has to be managed on an appropriate developmental timeline. We *must* be involved in the details, supporting the structures that are in place with wise counsel and guidance. The endgame is productive problem-solving.

What does this look like in practice? Clark University's Wendy Grolnick and her colleagues conducted an experiment that investigated 'parental provision of structure'.[1] They identified four specific components of effective structure development that parents can follow (as a pattern, not a formula) to guide children successfully.

Jointly established rules

Encouraging our children's input in the structures that will impact their lives can be a powerful way to do this well. When we invite our children's input, we become *involved* in the issue together. Considered and compassionate connection provides a firm foundation on which to make decisions. Inviting their input also supports competence. Asking 'What do you think?' demonstrates to a child that *we believe in their decision-making capability*, and that we feel they have the competence to make safe and healthy decisions.

We must consider the developmental appropriateness of a joint decision-making process. Our children's age, experience, and maturity will impact the degree to which their opinions and ideas influence our decisions. Allowing a 4-year-old to decide bedtime is potentially unwise (although many parents will be surprised at how effectively a child will self-regulate around sleep in the right environment). Giving a 9-year-old the determining voice in deciding what age a mobile phone should be given, what type of phone, and what apps to download for the phone is almost always unwise. (Self-regulation typically drops when screens are involved.) As parents we sometimes make decisions jointly with our children, and other times we seek our children's input but then make the decision ourselves. Context is everything.

Open exchange

For jointly established rules, there must be open communication about what the rules and expectations are. Our children won't always agree with what is decided. An autonomy-supportive approach to the development of structure must allow for disagreement. Sometimes we will listen to our children and respond positively. Other times, their criticisms of the rules and structures we're developing will be based on their immaturity and inexperience. This is where the third, vital dimension – empathy – applies.

Empathy

Decades of science tells us that parents who master the art of empathy tend to create an environment that supports needs better than those who don't. Seeing the world through our children's eyes – having the capacity to perceive their frame of reference – facilitates the most need-supportive conversations and decisions. Most boundaries, rules, limits, or structures that we develop are going to be uninteresting, unmotivating, or undesirable. After all, if they were interesting, motivating, and desirable, we wouldn't need to sit down and develop structures and boundaries for our children. The real challenge, therefore, is for us to sit with our children as we have some open exchange of ideas about structures for things like morning and evening routines, schoolwork or home duties, and try to find a mutually agreeable solution to something they often don't want to agree to. And that is where empathy plays a key role.

'Empathy,' according to researcher Brené Brown, 'fuels connection.'[2] She emphasises that when we're empathic, we take the perspective of the other person, stay out of judgment, recognise the other's emotion, and communicate those insights. It follows that we can say to our child, 'It doesn't seem fair. It's so hard. Wouldn't it be so good if we didn't have to have any rules.' We can even agree with our child: 'I know. We *all* wish we could do whatever we want!'

Establishing structures can be a tricky business. Empathy is a vital ingredient to help us move in the direction of autonomy-supportive, rather than controlling, decision-making.

Choice

Once a decision has been made about structure, we offer our children as much choice as we can (based on their age, experience, and maturity) so they can do things in a way that feels good for them. This is the big autonomy support element, right here. The structure that's been agreed to might be that piano practice is best done before dinner, but the child can choose exactly when that happens within that timeframe. The structure that's been agreed to could be that their bedroom is to be clean by bedtime, but when they do it is up to them, so long as that time target is met.

When we facilitate choice for our children, they're more likely to be interested, to persist, and to feel competent. We're supporting their need. And it bears highlighting: when children are involved in the design of their structures, it's easier for them to do what they say they're going to do.

Rules are rules

Lest anyone still think autonomy-supportive development of structure in a child's life means that parents are rolling over and acquiescing to everything a child wants in a permissive permutation of pathetic parenting, let's recognise a key truth: parents have an obligation to parent.

Implementing structure is an empathic and collaborative process that, when done well, ensures clarity and consistency of rules and expectations and offers clear reasons for the structures that have been agreed to. It also outlines predictable consequences in the event that choices are made to ignore the structures that are in place. And it places the parent in the role of leader in the exchange until children are developmentally capable of working more independently on their own preferences, rules, and structures.

Developing structure in an autonomy-supportive way is going to look different for toddlers and teens. Context is everything. Empathy remains present for all scenarios, but the way we jointly establish rules, exchange ideas, and give choice is also guided by factors like age, experience, and maturity. And gender, apparently: studies looking into how parents implement their structures have found we're more controlling with structure for boys than for girls. Perhaps this is because parents feel girls are more cooperative? Or more competent?

A 2015 study found that 'at every age, females were significantly higher in impulse control and lower in sensation-seeking' compared with males.[3] Other studies show that boys are more engaged in a task when more structure is offered. They like to know where the boundaries are, why they're there, and how to bump up against them. Boys tend to benefit more from having limits and requests clearly articulated. Girls engage more with metacognitive support, meaning they prefer emotional engagement and the opportunity to think through the learning process.[4]

This is important knowledge and it reinforces precisely what this chapter is about. Structure matters. But, as flagged, so does context. Taking into account our children's maturity, experience, age, gender, and development will help to create and implement structures that set them up for success.

Maria's tortillas are better than Alexa's because she's had the time to gain experience and develop competence. The same principle applies when it comes to children's behaviour with friends and family, learning at school, and contributions around the home. Allowing time to gain experience and providing structures that emphasise involvement with others, prosocial values, and reasonable and mutually agreed upon expectations will lead to the development of competence – because children will be more motivated to internalise the things we hope to teach them. Structure that is developed in autonomy-supportive ways provides a sense of certainty in our children. They feel in control. Structure minimises randomness, volatility, and unpredictability. And that's probably because structure, when it comes from an autonomy-supportive context, gets parents and kids involved in one another's worlds (creating connection and relatedness), and gives children a voice (creating autonomy), which makes them feel capable (creating competence).

10 The most powerful question in the world

You are the parent of a youngish child, aged somewhere around five or six years old. They want to do some colouring or painting. Do you:

a hand over the textas, paints, pencils, and paper, and say 'go for your life'?

b sit down with them and explain that paint and textas can make a big mess, so they need to only paint at the table, clean the brushes between painting different colours, point out how textas go through the paper so a placemat needs to be used, and run and get some cleaning gear? Or

c work out an option where they can paint, and you can feel comfortable knowing they're not going to mess everything up?

If that scenario doesn't resonate because your children are older, you can apply these options to almost any parenting scenario. Your child wants to be on social media or a digital game. They want to have a sleepover with friends. They're heading to the park to play – or a party on Saturday night. They want to leave high school and go on a school-leavers party trip with their friends for a week.

In each scenario, taking option a is to be permissive. We essentially say, 'Fill your boots!' and hand them the keys to the proverbial car. There's a lack of involvement, and no structure to facilitate competence building.

Option b means we choose control. The extremely caricatured version of this is 'Not on my watch', or 'If I say yes, it's going to be done my way. It's my house. These are my rules.' Involvement is high but restrictive. Structures are put in place but autocratically and unilaterally, by the parent. This controlling approach ignores your child's perspective and voice, and it minimises your child's opportunity to grow. It also demonstrates a stunning lack of trust in your child's capacity to learn, grow, and develop.

Option c? It's obviously the one I'm going to point to as the example of high-quality parenting. But why? Let's examine this with a real-life experiment (and note that this example is not about painting as much as it's about principles).

Richard Koestner, a Canadian researcher, teamed up with Richard Ryan to investigate how control and autonomy affect children. The situation? An art class.[1] In their study, first- and second- graders were divided into groups and told they would be participating in a painting project. Rules were established for the children to follow while doing their art. The children were told that being neat and tidy mattered. Staying in the lines was important. Brushes were to be rinsed when swapping from one paint colour to another. Other rules were put in place so the children knew the purpose of the activity and how it was to be assessed. But it was the way these rules were established that sets up this experiment. One group of children experienced limits being set in an autonomy-*restrictive* manner. Here, the adults explained the rules to the children, lecture style. The other group of children established their rules with the adults in a collaborative way. Their set-up was autonomy-*supportive*.

Before we get to the findings, consider how this autonomy-restrictive approach affects children's other basic psychological needs. When someone is correcting and directing, children are unlikely to feel seen, heard, and valued. The level of connection and relatedness is low. It also sends a message about competence. When children are being told all of the rules in a controlling way, the overarching signal is one that says 'I don't believe in you. You can't do this without my oversight.' Competence needs are damaged.

The findings will, therefore, be no surprise. Setting limits in a controlling and dictatorial way reduced the children's intrinsic motivation for the painting activity, and it also resulted in less creative art being produced by the kids. Comparatively, an autonomy-supportive approach to setting limits (which got the same results in terms of neatness and cleanliness) led to increased motivation and creativity on the part of the children in that group. The autonomy-supportive approach (i) is about collaborative problem-solving within reasonable limits with parental/adult guidance, and (ii) gets better outcomes than controlling approaches.

Autonomy

By now you probably have a reasonably strong sense of what autonomy support is. The past four chapters have outlined the effectiveness of need-supportive parenting, reviewed our children's three basic psychological needs, and identified that we can be supportive or restrictive in the way we meet our children's relatedness and competence needs. Supportive approaches work best. At the heart of the way we support our children's needs is the process of autonomy support.

We've also identified that an autonomy-supportive approach involves:

- taking perspective

- encouraging and supporting your child's voice

- offering meaningful rationales for behavioural requests

- providing appropriate and meaningful choices where possible, and

- minimising controlling language.

In this chapter we get to the heart of the need-supportive parenting style. We explore autonomy and how we support it.

They're good rules

I share the following experience (from 2015) about my eldest daughter, Chanel, with her permission. Chanel, aged 16 years and 11 months, is late for work. 'Dad, come on! I need to go!' I trudge out to our dark blue 2003 Toyota Corolla Sportivo Hatch and ease into the passenger seat. Chanel is in the driver's seat, engine running. Lately Chanel is always driving, trying to accrue the minimum hours required in her learner logbook so she can sit the test for her driver's licence one month from now. Her learner plates are displayed on the front and rear bumpers of the car, tightly held in place as a signal to other drivers that she's under instruction.

Chanel pushes the clutch to the floor, shifts the gearstick to first, lifts her left foot off the clutch and accelerates out of the street. Work is only two kilometres away, but she drives like she's in a rally car. First, second, third, fourth, fifth, and then sixth gear, revs high. I remind her of the speed limit and she slows down, but she scowls as she does so.

'You okay?' I ask. No response.

I pause. The *I'm mad at you and so I'm not talking to you* vibes are emanating from her, but I can't work out why. Tentatively I reach out with my next question. 'I'm guessing that right now you're upset and, while I'm not sure why, I think you might be upset with me. Am I reading this right?'

The car surges as she turns a corner and accelerates back to the speed limit. A long pause. Then, 'Yes. I am mad at you.' Silence.

'I'm trying to think of what I could have done to leave you feeling so upset. But I'm coming up blank. I feel like things have been good lately. Would you be comfortable sharing why you're mad?'

I wait. The last intersection before her workplace is ahead of us. Red lights. As the car comes to a standstill my cranky almost-17-year-old sighs, shifts the car back into first, and angrily responds. 'Fine. Two weeks ago everyone went to a party but they didn't invite me and I didn't even know it was on. But today they accidentally mentioned it, and when I asked why I wasn't invited they told me that they kept it a secret because it was the kind of party that Dr Justin Coulson wouldn't approve of.' She glowers at me, sadness and frustration combining with adolescent pain and isolation.

I know I need to get this right. Stay calm. Show empathy and understanding. See the world through her eyes. But also ensure she knows there are good reasons for our rules. The car moves forward as the lights change. I have about 45 seconds until we're at her work. Can I say what needs to be said in that timeframe?

'You must have felt terrible. I can see how much it's hurt you.' A softening in her eyes. 'I'm really grateful you were willing to tell me that while you're still so upset. It's hard to have these conversations sometimes.'

We're turning into the driveway of her workplace. The clock is ticking. 'I'd love to talk with you about it if you've got time. Work doesn't start for a few minutes yet.'

Chanel parks the car and stops the engine. Silence.

'Fine.'

'So ... I'm so sad for you and I know it's hard. But if I'm honest, I'm kind of glad you weren't at that party two weeks ago. I'm guessing that there was alcohol there. And other drugs. And there were probably kids disappearing into bedrooms or cars or bushes and having intimate experiences with other people that they'd be likely to regret the next day.'

'Yes.' A pause as she calibrates her thoughts. 'But, Dad. It's not fair. We've got all these rules, and I'm being excluded because I'm different. I'm the only one whose parents won't let them go to parties because there's alcohol. And I'm not going to do anything wrong.'

I reply, gently, 'This is hard for me. I want to keep you safe. And those rules … that structure we've developed … we've done it together. You've made those rules with me. We've talked about these rules and these ideas. I've asked you what you think is the best thing to do so you can be safe and healthy. You've worked out these rules with me. I haven't forced them on you … but I can see it's getting trickier.

'You'll be an adult in about 13 months,' I continue. 'I won't have any input into your decisions at all then, unless you ask for it. And I hoped that the rules we've created would be able to be the rules until that time and beyond. But maybe we need to have a conversation about the rules. Now … I don't want to change them. You've told me they're good rules. I think they're good rules. What do you think?'

We sit in silence for an uncomfortably long time. The sun is setting, and I'm watching stunning yellows, pinks, and purples colour the sky as I wait for a response. Finally, 'Dad, I don't like the rules. Not one bit.'

My heart sinks. My mind races, searching for a wise response that will rescue my daughter from the danger I can feel her racing towards. Nothing comes to me. I open my mouth to speak but think better of it.

Chanel continues. 'I really don't like the rules at all.' More silence. Then: 'But, Dad. They're good rules. I think we should keep them.'

At this point I'm almost certain that the heavens open and the angels sing in chorus, 'Hallelujah!' She squeezes my hand and climbs out of the car. 'See you at nine o'clock.' And she's gone.

How did we get there? What happened to lead my daughter to make that choice that night? It was need-supportive parenting. Involvement. Structure. And autonomy.

Supporting autonomy

Ask a scholar what autonomy means and they'll say something like:

> Autonomy is a form of functioning associated with feeling
> volitional, congruent, and integrated … when acting with
> autonomy, behaviours are engaged wholeheartedly, whereas
> one experiences incongruence and conflict when doing
> what is contrary to one's volition.[2]

When I think about a definition like this and apply it to parenting, I get nervous. It makes me think of a toddler or preschooler (or worse, *a teenager!*) doing what he wants. And in some ways, this is accurate. But not entirely. Look carefully. There's more to that Ed Deci/Richard Ryan definition of autonomy than self-focused gratification.

Volition alone might be about doing what feels good. But words like 'congruent' and 'integrated' suggest that values also play a part in autonomy. Being wholehearted suggests that something must *feel right* to be engaged in autonomously. It's deeper than doing what you want. It's doing what you want in alignment with your sense of identity and your values. It's acting congruously.

What it's really saying is that autonomy is making choices about what you're going to do based on the deep end of the motivation continuum. Autonomy is making decisions that aren't based on what someone says you have to do (external regulation), or what you feel like you 'must' do (introjected regulation). It's not based on what you figure is 'right' (identified regulation). Instead it's about doing what you're doing because it's a reflection of your values and who you are (integrated regulation) and because you *want* to (intrinsic regulation).

This is a lofty ambition. We're trying to get our kids there? How?

To support autonomy, we literally become 'autonomy supportive'. But, again, this must be emphasised: autonomy-supportive parenting is *not* permissiveness; it's *not* taking our hands off the parenting steering wheel and giving unfettered freedom to our children. It's *not* giving our children supreme independence, dusting off our hands and saying, 'Figure it out yourself, kid.' That's called abrogating our responsibility as parents ... which is *not* autonomy supportive; in fact it's neglect. Permissiveness means there are no structures in the form of guidelines, rules, and expectations. Neglect means no involvement. Autonomy support clearly incorporates both structure and involvement.

Then there's the developmental reality to consider. A consistent theme that we'll return to again now is that our children are entirely dependent on us when they're young, and although they will develop and grow – and thus rely on us less in some things as they mature – dependence remains throughout their childhood and adolescence. They're not supposed to be independently choosing until they have the maturity and experience to do that. The way we support autonomy for a 2-year-old or a 5-year-old is quite different to the way we support autonomy for an adolescent. As our children develop the capacity to think through consequences and engage with ideas and principles, we alter our parenting accordingly. We think about where they're at in their maturity, identity development and understanding of values, and adapt accordingly. Autonomy support means we are involved in our children's development.

What characterises a healthy parent–child relationship is 'autonomous dependence' at the growing edge of our children's development. While apparently contradictory, the term neatly captures that 'I love you, go away' energy toddlers (and teens) exhibit when they're striding out but wanting to stay connected with or in sight of their parent. At every age, as they seek to acquire new skills and capabilities, they'll ideally turn to us for guidance. Their reliance on us will occur most often when they see that we support their competence and their autonomy. They want and need us to be the guide on the side.

Autonomy support means judging how much to guide our children's growth by helping them make safe, healthy decisions. Autonomy-supportive parents reduce the extent to which they make decisions for their child, which would be autonomy restrictive. Rather, autonomy support means we give our children the opportunity to experience choosing, and embrace their choices as their own, having *ownership* over both choices and outcomes. If a problem needs to be solved, we don't leave it to them to solve it. Instead, we help them to develop solutions, encouraging them to take the lead in a developmentally appropriate way. But, depending on their age, they may need a lot of guidance and – you guessed it – support to make safe, healthy, wise decisions. So, we provide scaffolding and structure along with deep involvement.

When does this parenting start? Early. Wendy Grolnick showed that 1-year-olds respond one way to autonomy supportive parents and another way to controlling parents. Guy Roth and Avi Assor, two Israeli researchers who examine need support in parenting and in schools, have found that children respond better – and experience more functional outcomes – to autonomy supportive parents and teachers at all ages. Belgian researchers Maarten van Steenkiste and Bart Soenens have identified that teens are more likely to make healthier, safer choices with less control and more autonomy support. At every age and stage, the story appears the same. The earlier we start, the better. But the way we do it has to be guided by our children.

Why is autonomy support superior? This returns us to my statement in Chapter 7 that autonomy support is the linchpin of high-quality parenting.

Autonomy support meets relatedness needs. You cannot support autonomy without establishing respectful involvement, because it requires seeing the world through your child's eyes and understanding what matters to them.

Autonomy support also meets competence needs, because you can't offer autonomy without showing that you believe in your child's ability to work things out.

This is the part I want to shout from the rooftops!

The elegance and inter-connectedness of this need-supportive approach to raising children is sublime. When we *work with* our children, using non-controlling involvement and non-controlling development of structure, rather than *doing things to* our children, using controlling and restrictive involvement and structure, we create an environment that supports their needs.[3] As we puzzle through any problem-solving process that autonomy support *supports*, we shift our children from shallow external motivation into the deeper forms of motivation, which include identified, integrated, and intrinsic motivation. It's harder than permissively shrugging our shoulders and walking away. It's far more challenging than putting our foot down and controlling the situation so things work out *our* way. But the hard work is worth it. The results consistently point in a positive direction.

A note: Some parents think autonomy support means we facilitate our children's choice in *everything*. This isn't practical, however idealistic it might be. The younger our children are, the fewer decisions they'll make. As they develop, they'll have more problems to solve, more opportunities to think about choices, and more capacity to work with you through decisions. Even so, we don't need to make *every* decision – from what they wear to what they eat or when they go to sleep or who they play with – into an autonomy-supportive process. More is generally better, but quality is important. This doesn't have to be a painstaking procession of conversations to endure for the 20 years you're raising your child.

Autonomy support trusts the process

You must be thinking: if autonomy support is so awesome, then why is it so hard to do?

Here are some possible answers to that question:

- The models we have around us are permissive or controlling. Parents, teachers, bosses, the government … most people with power either ignore us or tell us what to do all the time. We don't see autonomy support in too many contexts and it is hard to be what you cannot see.

- Our parents were unlikely to have been concerned with our basic psychological needs. There's a societal expectation that we'll parent in these less functional ways because that's how it's always been done. Culture is strong.

- The more controlling forms of parenting make it look like we're parent-ing *more* and parenting *harder* than an autonomy-supportive approach. If we care about how other people perceive us, it will be hard to move into a need-supportive approach, particularly in the early stages of trying it out.

- These controlling and permissive types of parenting are easier, faster, and require less effort. We don't need to practise perspective-taking or compassion when we're controlling our children's every choice or shrugging our shoulders in a vaguely permissive mindset.

- Autonomy support requires time on our part, and as we experience more pressure with work and family commitments, we have less time and less psychological availability to spend in autonomy-supportive processes with our children.

- Adult mental health issues are increasing, and these reduce our capacity to be present, engaged, and fully functional in developing structure to guide our children successfully.

- Our ego gets in the way. We feel like our children's positive outcomes are entirely our responsibility and so we control more.

There's one more reason that, as parents, we default to less effective parenting styles. It's one word: Trust.

Trust and pressure

In the Introduction and elsewhere in this book, I have described the increasingly relentless pressure parents and children are experiencing. Control is up. Autonomy is down. Self-determination is primarily allowed only when it's consistent with parental wishes, which hardly counts as autonomy support. Children are under pressure to become high achievers, to do well, to maximise their potential (whatever that means ... I'm still yet to maximise mine, so I don't know how our 7- or 16-year-old kids are supposed to achieve this feat).

Parents are in broad agreement: today our society has become more competitive than ever before. The pressure our children feel comes from us, from themselves, from schools. It's almost like it permeates everything – like it comes from the very air they breathe. Our neoliberalist meritocracy has created a culture that demands unrealistic standards of success and achievement – for both us and our children. It's driven the intensification and fetishisation of parenting that I described in the early chapters of this book. Moreover, today's parents carry a burden most of our parents didn't know existed: that if our children cannot successfully navigate the increasingly competitive world in which we live, it's not just their failure. *It's ours as well.* Many of us feel a need for our children to succeed – for their own sake, but for ours too. Our ego is involved in how they turn out. And that's a precarious place to live. The result is that we step in. We don't trust that the outcome will take care of itself. We show conditional parental regard. Control.

The high-pressure society our kids are immersed in presents a dangerous script that many of us follow, *even if we disagree with it*. Many of us want to resist and react against the brutality of a competitive 'push, push, push; more, more, more' societal norm … but instead, we acquiesce. We even elevate the script. Some of us harangue our children to get their grades up so they can attend selective or specialist public schools or the fancy private school we've heard so much about. After-school tutoring is a booming industry, and other extracurricular, structured activities are as popular as ever.[4]

This rise of pressure and the corresponding parental expectations regarding their children's achievements across the industrialised world are, according to psychologists, 'at extremes that are cause for concern'.[5] That's the sort of sentence I want to say again, IN CAPS, for emphasis:

> The pressure-filled lives we and our children are living
> are 'AT EXTREMES THAT ARE CAUSE FOR
> CONCERN'.

Too many kids are living with too much pressure to perform, and with that pressure comes control – and a frustrated and thwarted need for autonomy. It also takes its toll on those two other needs: relationships suffer, and kids consistently feel incompetent; like what they do is never good enough. This in turn breeds anxiety and perfectionism – both, incidentally, on the rise for 20–30 years now.

Dr Thomas Curran is a psychology researcher from the London School of Economics who studies perfectionism. According to Curran, 'Pressure to raise successful children in a culture that emphasises monetary wealth and social standing has … consequences for the behaviour of parents.' Those consequences? When parents feel this pressure, regardless of its source, we're more likely to adopt more anxious and overly controlling parenting styles.[6] The higher the stakes, the greater the control. We push our children into pathways that may not be aligned with their interests and desires. And we become increasingly involved in their routines, activities, and emotions. Involvement is good – but only when it's autonomy-supportive involvement. According to Curran's critique, we're seeing autonomy-*restrictive* parenting practices on- the rise, particularly in the way we're *involved* with our children. Meanwhile autonomy-*supportive* practices are dropping off. In large part, our increasingly competitive, high-stakes societal scripts are the reason.

In summary: high stakes = high control. It makes me cringe to say, but I need to make it explicit. The message that control sends to our children is this:

I don't trust you.

Control is really about trust – or lack of it. The more controlling we are, the more we're telling our children that we don't trust them. As you read this, perhaps you're taken aback. Maybe you're pretty certain that you do trust your child. But … is that true? How sure are you? Do we believe that our children are designed to develop optimally (in the right environment)? Or do we feel like we need to force their development, shape it, curate it? Think back to the mums in Grolnick's study of 1-year-olds. Consider the parents in

Ed Deci's study of older children. A large percentage of them felt as though they needed to force their child's hand. They had to take control, 'help' their child succeed. Push them to do each task 'the right way'. And in the process, they showed a lack of trust in their child's innate desire for mastery.

The more we control, the more we lack trust in that intrinsic developmental capability our children are born with. Every other species on the planet trusts that its young will develop naturally and healthily. The mumma and dadda birds, fish, reptiles, and animals don't harass their offspring for not vocalising, walking, flying, or swimming early enough. They put them in the right environment, support them, and trust they'll develop. And, sure enough, it happens. Meanwhile, those parents provide support for their needs. They're involved. They provide boundaries/structure. It works. (Of course, they're not pushing them into a cutthroat school system and job market ... Nature isn't exactly friendly though, is it?)[7]

If we're going to support autonomy effectively, trust is *the* critical element. And not just any kind of trust. This isn't the sort of trust where you can leave your child in the kitchen with the bowl of lollies and feel confident they won't eat any. I'm talking about trust in our child's intrinsic growth tendencies and preferences for good. If we trust in our children's built-in desire to grow and develop as our philosophical starting point in parenting, from here on we simply need to support their needs and our children *will* develop well. They may err. Now and then they might completely mess up. But because of the intrinsic tendencies for growth that are within them, they'll steer back towards that need-supportive environment we're providing (with involvement, structure, and autonomy support) and they'll exhibit a desire to grow and develop optimally and functionally in that environment. It's a matter of trust. When they feel our trust, their tendency will be to shy away from environments that don't support those needs in healthy ways – which helps to explain why kids who are struggling but who have controlling parents tend to minimise their time in the family environment and find other environments in which to develop instead. (Incidentally, this trust in their intrinsic growth tendencies gives us the permission we need to be less over-the-top, because we trust that our kids have in-built developmental capacity.)

Trust means that we believe:

- Children are naturally built so that they *want* to master their environment.

- It's a natural process for our children to internalise our values, behaviours, and attitudes.

External pressure and control works against these natural developmental tendencies that our children have, that steer them towards growth and goodness.[8]

Parents who trust in a healthy, natural development process typically step away from controlling interactions with their infants, and instead let their little ones lead the way. They're involved and responsive, but not controlling. Autonomy-supportive mothers are more relaxed about developmental milestones and are less likely to compare their child's progress and development to that of other children. Importantly, this trust in healthy and natural development is *negatively* associated with permissive parenting. This means that as trust in the child's ability to develop adaptively and functionally increases, parents are *less* likely to be permissive or laissez faire. Rather, they remain positively engaged and involved, but their presence is supportive rather than controlling.

How development works

Psychologists have observed that many of us have a false idea that development happens in a straightforward, linear fashion. We expect that our children will mature from A to B at around the same time as their same-age peers. But the ages at which individual children achieve developmental milestones typically varies enormously. Speech is an example. Some kids say their first words by around nine months of age. Others don't say anything until some months after their second birthday. Yet both will generally develop speech and language capabilities that are indistinguishable later in life. Development isn't linear. It regularly stalls for extended periods of time. Sometimes there's regression. A child goes from walking back to crawling. A child goes from managing big emotions well to breaking down constantly over trivialities. A child is a bundle of empathy at age 9 and has no empathy at age 15. All of this is normal.

Understanding this helps us to trust that our children will mature and develop to healthy functionality in their own time. This knowledge reduces pressure – which as we now know is associated with controlling/restrictive behaviour, i.e. is undesirable – and promotes parenting that allows the child's natural growth processes to play out. Parents who trust in the process will be less stressed –

and so will their kids. Rigid expectations about age and maturation milestones undermine that trust and reduce responsiveness and healthy involvement.

This can be tough when your child is 'falling behind' or has received a diagnosis related to neurological or psychological challenges. Chapter 11 will address those additional difficulties.

A parenting 'blue zone'

In a 2008 study, researchers compared Norwegian and Canadian mothers, and discovered that culture plays a role in how much we trust our children to develop healthily, and how much autonomy support we provide. When Norwegian mothers completed their surveys, the data showed they enjoyed good basic psychological need support in their role as mums. They felt like they had good relationships and a sense of belonging in society, support for their development as parents, and plenty of autonomy in their motherhood choices. Their needs were supported at a societal level. It was kind of like that 'it takes a village' idea was working in their favour. Perhaps as a flow-on, these Norwegian mothers were trusting of their child's development and were well able to support their child's basic psychological needs through positive involvement and structure provision. (Mothers who had partners and husbands providing support for their needs were also highly likely to be trusting and lean towards these positive outcomes.) Canadian mothers scored significantly lower in the degree to which they experienced their needs being met at a societal level. And they trusted less in their children's natural developmental processes. They were far more stressed and pressured about parenting expectations.

What does this mean? Should we all move to Scandinavian countries because the social support and belief in healthy development is so strong? Do we just need to find supportive partners?

Globally, there are a handful of 'blue zones': locations in which people live longer, healthier lives compared with the rest of the world. The reason for these blue zones? Culture. People there live differently to the rest of us. If you were to move to one of these blue zones, you'd likely adopt the behaviours of the people around you, and therefore experience the same health benefits and positive aging opportunities.

I've touched on this several times in different ways throughout this book, but let's get really explicit: if culture is 'what everyone does around here', the current first-world parenting culture is one of anxiety, intensity, pressure, and control. Parents want to mitigate risk and guarantee success outcomes for their children. Intensity, restriction, and pressure become the *modus operandi*. This is associated with more controlling parenting, and therefore, greater frustration of children's basic psychological needs.

We're not all moving to Norway! Instead, we have to create (or find) our parenting 'blue zone'. Is there a place we can go, or a place we can build, where the culture is one of autonomy support and trust in our children's innate healthy developmental processes rather than control and autonomy restriction? Trying to do it alone can be tough. A community that walks in the same direction has far more strength.

The holy grail

Let's run with the idea that every parent's dream is to turn out children who are inclined to do the right thing at the right time for the right reasons *without* parents having to be monitoring them all the time, offering guidance, correction, and direction. For many of us, achieving that feels about as likely as finding fairies at the bottom of the garden. They do actually need us – but for support and gentle guidance, not a stream of constant correction and direction.

If we revisit my experience with my daughter in the car that evening as we drove to work, we can imagine how she might have reacted if I'd chosen a controlling, restrictive approach. Say my response to her complaint was, 'If you don't like the rules, tough luck. They're there for your own good.' She may have been compliant towards me in our conversation, but it's likely that the next day at school she'd have told her friends she expected an invite to the next party, and it's probable that she'd have lied to me when that party was happening so she could go without interrogation. Our relationship would have been hurt.

But here's the hard thing to admit about that conversation – and I share it with her permission. Despite our autonomy-supportive interaction and the apparent positive outcome we achieved, her response was still at the shallow end of the motivation continuum. I didn't know it at the time, but eventually I found out that her answer was an introjected response. She was saying it because she felt as though she had to. She needed to. She didn't want me to police her, but she was policing herself from the inside in a way that was out of step with her developing identity. Over the subsequent 24 months, my daughter made personal choices that were inconsistent with her assurance and statement that 'They're good rules, Dad. I think we should keep them.'

I experienced challenges as I grappled with the difference between *conditional parental regard* and *unconditional parental regard*. I had to learn to love my daughter. No. Matter. What. Even when my values were put away and she chose, as an adult, to make decisions inconsistent with what I wanted for her.

It made me wonder, am I a good parent? Was I a good parent when my daughter was compliant but, with her personal decisions at odds with my values, did that make me a bad parent? If I was not a good parent, at what point did I stop being a good parent? Was it the first time she felt compelled to comply with a direction she disagreed with? What was it? When did my worthiness as a parent shift from good to bad?

As I've already explained, the 'Am I a good parent?' question is unhelpful at best, and destructive at worst. We all want to know if we're good parents. But what metric do we use? If it's how our children turn out and their decisions and the outcomes of those decisions, the metric is a subjective mess.[9]

My daughter sat in the car with me that night, outside her work, and reflected on the choices she had before her. I'd reminded her of the involved discussions we'd had, developing structures designed 'by her' (or with her acquiescence to parental expectations) to stay safe and healthy. I'd provided her the space she needed to think for herself and determine her own choices. In that moment of decision, her response had been 'They're good rules.' That night, I drove home convinced that her choice was as close to parenting's holy grail as you can get. Perhaps, in that moment, it was.

But values shift and change, particularly during adolescence. Introjected motivation isn't as durable as identification and integration. As a parent who wants to be a 'good' parent, I later discovered I had a new challenge: to work through my disappointment. Moreover, I had to identify where I could have made different statements to move past the introject.

When I tell this story, people often ask, 'What would you have done if she said she *didn't* like the rules?' For a short period, that became the reality. And it led to something new. It was something painful. And it stretched me. I learned that in parenting, there is no magic recipe or formula. It's a hard role to fill.

But when challenges arise, we either stagnate, regress, or grow. I choose growth.

When she chose alternate rules, it meant acknowledging that my disappointment was mine rather than blaming her for my sorrow. It meant asking questions like, What can we do differently? How can we help our child understand that she's still loved, no matter what? And how can we help our child to engage in a process where she's continuing to grow, even if her choices aren't consistent with our own?

What would I have done if she said she didn't like the rules? I would have struggled. And I would have loved her in spite of it all.

11

Complex needs

According to the Australian Institute of Health and Welfare (AIHW), in 2013–14, an estimated 314,000 children aged 4–11 [almost 14%] experienced a mental disorder.[1]

We're talking primary-school-aged kids here, and we're looking at about one in seven kids. That's about 4 in every classroom across the nation, on average. The AIHW data indicate that boys were more commonly affected than girls (17% compared with 11%). Attention-deficit/hyperactivity disorder (ADHD) ranked as the top disorder for this age group (8.2%), and it was the number one diagnosis for boys (11% were diagnosed). Next most diagnosed: anxiety disorders, with 6.9% of all primary school-aged children experiencing a clinical diagnosis. Girls were more likely to experience anxiety disorder (6.1%) than boys.

Adolescent data based on information collected from parents/carers in the Young Minds Matter survey showed 'an estimated 245,000 of our teens (around 14%) experienced a mental disorder in the 12 months before the survey, with a higher proportion of males than females (16% compared with 13%).' Anxiety and ADHD were the most common disorders (7.0% and 6.3%, respectively). These disorders split along gender lines for older children in the same way they did for younger children, with 7.7% of girls experiencing anxiety and 9.8% of boys with an ADHD diagnosis.[2]

These data are the best we have at time of writing – they give the fullest picture – but they're nearly a decade old and will only have been amplified in the intervening years. A spike is anticipated thanks to the Covid-19 pandemic and the mental health implications associated with extended government lockdowns and restrictions. But independent of Covid-related issues, children and adolescent rates of depression, perfectionism, obsessive-compulsive disorder (OCD), autism, oppositional defiant disorder (ODD), sensory processing disorder (SPD), pathological demand avoidance (PDA), and more have been climbing.

Children who experience these conditions present parents with a range of challenges that make the already tough job of parenting even tougher. If we look at ADHD as an example, we see a child who has attentional issues, where self-regulation and inhibition are low and impulsivity or inattention are high. These children are likely to:

Struggle with school

Note, they don't have an intelligence problem. They have a focus and inhibition problem, so they typically get lower grades.

Struggle with friends

Kids with these challenging behaviours are the ones who miss out on birthday parties, sleepovers, bike rides in the neighbourhood, and so on. They don't inhibit themselves all that well (unless they've also got anxiety): they talk over people, they talk too much, and their communication is often overdone in their desperate attempts to make and keep friends.

Struggle with family relationships

Tired, stressed, 'over it' parents sometimes do and say things that leave them feeling lousy. Siblings can be unkind too.

Struggle with big emotions

When inhibition and regulation are your kryptonite, big emotions like anger, frustration, disappointment, and anxiety get really intense, and they're hard to control, often impacting family relationships, friendships, schooling, and so on.

Struggle with big behaviours

Impulsivity and inattention mean that if a child with ADHD finds anything uninteresting, they're going to want to move on. As they have poor tolerance for 'boring stuff', they generally want something else NOW. If anything blocks their exit, lack of inhibition combined with big emotions can mean explosive behaviour.

Struggle with self-esteem

When they're constantly questioning their competence (or having the significant adults and peers in their life question their competence), kids with ADHD question their worth. This increases their risk of depression, anxiety, and other 'comorbidities'.

The list goes on, but you get the picture. Life isn't easy for these kids or for their parents and teachers. We could make a similar list for every child who has any additional need.

Here's the problem: most parents I speak with tell me that their doctors, paediatricians, and psychologists and psychiatrists advise them to become more controlling in order to make their families function more effectively. Autonomy support rarely, if ever, enters the conversation.

Perhaps a more generous reporting is: parents are told to implement a variety of external contingencies. The remedy is punishments and rewards – so we're playing in the shallow end of the motivation continuum, where children are expected to behave for rewards, or to avoid consequences. The promise is that the parents can have peace and harmony in their home. Parents are encouraged to use reward charts, praise, and other forms of verbal 'doggy biscuits' to increase compliance. They're expected to withhold privileges and use time-out when behaviour doesn't align with parental demands. Set the limit. Establish the boundary. Let the kid know what's required and hold firm.

And most parents tell me they hate it. (Which is usually why they make the effort to find me.) Based on what we've covered thus far in the book, you can probably tell *me* why, but here's my brief explanation.

The motivation continuum

If we return to the extrinsic/intrinsic motivational continuum in Chapter 6, we immediately see that this typical expert-approved approach is a problem. It's all about one specific kind of motivation: external motivation, which is the least helpful kind. Yet it's by far and away the dominant approach that parents are encouraged to use by so many mental health and healthcare professionals. And many parents feel that they can't get their children to do *anything* without the threat of punishment or the promise of a reward. In other words, they agree that these approaches are the only things that 'work'.

Alfie Kohn is the author of several powerful and provocative books on parenting, including *Punished by Rewards*. In a podcast discussion with me, Kohn explained:

> Intrinsic motivation means you do something because
> you want to do it, because you get a kick out of it.
> It's satisfying. Extrinsic motivation is where you do
> something to avoid a punishment or to get a reward. And
> what we know from research as well as experience is that
> the two tend to be inversely related. So the child who
> seems 'motivated to do it' in order to get the gold star …
> has more extrinsic motivation and as a direct result is now
> less committed to being a helpful person, less interested
> in whether his actions around the house are making other
> people feel good … so when parents say … 'they work', I
> always ask 'Work to do what?' 'What's your goal?' You can

get mindless obedience in the short run if the reward is juicy enough or the punishment is awful enough. What you can never get is a child who is happy, more ethical, more compassionate or caring, more of an independent thinker. All of the things we parents want in the long-term, rewards like star charts ... actually get in the way of our more ambitious long-term goals.

In other words, controlling parenting – the type that's endemic in our culture and that's specifically advocated for children with additional needs, often impacting family relationships, friendships, schooling, and so on – is precisely the type of parenting that moves children away from intrinsic motivation. An autonomy-supportive approach encourages the outcomes we want. It's just that it's harder when your kids have these additional needs. More on that soon.

Additional needs for parents

Often we forget that kids might not be the only ones who have additional needs. Our own mental health and stress is also a consideration. A parent with anxiety or depression (or maybe who's simply having a bad day) may read the opening chapter of this book, reflect on what it means to be a good parent, and perhaps immediately feel like a failure. What if mental health difficulties mean that you are too impacted, psychologically, to take your children to the museum, to the zoo, on a holiday, or even to the beach or park on the weekend? Activities like these are markers of 'good parenting', aren't they? What does it mean if they're out of reach for you?

In a podcast interview with author Anna Spargo-Ryan, a mother who's suffered with depression, anxiety and major psychopathy throughout her life, she lamented, 'How could I call myself a mother if I couldn't take [my kids] to a nearby play centre without having a panic attack in the car park?' In her memoir, *A Kind of Magic,* Anna described the way her anxiety affected her to the extent that she'd be trying to take her children somewhere, but then be so overwhelmed by the psychological cost that she'd pull over on the side of the road and sit in the car, 'waiting for the adrenaline to wear off. All the times every part of me was shouting: "Yes! I want to do all these things with you!" and I still said, "No".'

The pain of letting children down for reasons that feel out of your control is surely going to undermine your feelings of worthiness as a parent. But it also has the potential to reduce your capacity to function the way you want to – in an autonomy-supportive manner. It's hard to have that warm, nurturing, involved relationship when you're filled with sadness, guilt, and anger. It's almost impossible to encourage your child to push boundaries and take risks to build competence and support autonomy when your anxiety is overwhelming and you don't want to let your child out of your sight. The pressure builds. And the need to control things increases. Parenting is tough enough, but parenting with your own mental health challenges or additional needs, or parenting when your child has additional needs, is even tougher.

How privilege works in parenting

For any parent reading this book – but particularly for a parent who's grappling with mental health challenges, diagnoses, or other difficulties (either their own or their child's) – there's a real problem. Autonomy-supportive parenting seems so easy to read about but so hard to do. And the unfairness of life is that some people don't have as far to go as others to even place themselves on the starting grid.

Maybe it feels like you're reading a book by a guy who has a whole lot of answers and seems to be all across this parenting thing while you're (perhaps) struggling and wondering what it all really means and how to pull it together. Maybe it would help you to know a bit more about how I got to this point.

I went to uni in my late 20s and studied full-time for eight and a half years, determined to understand parenting to its depths (I lectured for a couple of years as well).

Since the early 2000s I've been researching, writing, studying, practising, and teaching the stuff in this book.

I've had six kids to practise on.

I don't have any mental health concerns.

I have a phenomenally supportive wife (we've been married since the late 1990s) who's done the overwhelming majority of the parenting while I've been out and about teaching others how it's done.

That same phenomenally supportive wife has also done the overwhelming majority of *everything* associated with supporting our family (and me) in the home while I've worked outside the home, which is a tremendous weight for her, and a remarkable release for me.

I'm as determined as ever to understand the fine-grained details of parenting – and to parent well. For example, I've recorded podcast interviews with world-leading authorities on these topics.

While I've almost failed to make house repayments more times than I can count (because it's been a challenging road), I've always had the security of a house – and an extended family who promised support if things got too tough. Economic security has been hard won, but we've had it.

None of my children have major mental health (or physical health) issues. We've had some problems, like many families, but we haven't had to overcome some of the big challenges some families grapple with.

What I'm getting at is that, while life hasn't been without its challenges – and it has been a bumpy road with plenty of sacrifice along the way – I'm aware of my privilege. I'm also aware there are so many things people are encountering that can make this parenting book seem hard – even impossible.

I don't want to project a sense of effortlessness when it comes to raising kids. Parenting can try us to our limits.

The need-supportive parenting principles in this book are often even more demanding of us when we're fighting against a backdrop of a culture that disagrees with these approaches, combined with a child's additional needs, our own mental health challenges, family members who say we're not being 'tough enough' on the kids; and then there's the GPs or psychologists who are pushing for reward charts, time-out, or some other controlling process. We struggle through financial demands that are creating more stress than we can handle, issues at school with our kids' friends or a teacher, job insecurity, a partner who isn't on the same page (or who isn't safe, or who drinks too much or games too much), and more.

This is in addition to all of us living in a world that isn't designed for kids. Our world pushes children into artificial environments (that are a modern invention designed for adult convenience) and those environments consistently undermine children's basic psychological needs of relatedness, competence, and autonomy. That same society and culture forces *us* into similar artificial environments (that are a modern invention designed for capitalism's convenience) and undermines our basic psychological needs too. There's noise pollution, air pollution, food that isn't really food filling our supermarkets, screen pollution, lack of sleep, and a host of other challenges that all undermine what this book is trying to encourage: a healthy approach to parenting and family life that supports the basic psychological needs of our kids and ourselves!

Unintended consequences

Since Chapter 1, I've been asking you to think about what makes a good parent and how you know if you're a good parent. Now I have to alert you to something: following the ideas in a book like this is a risk. You might try to be a need-supportive parent by following the steps so you can be a 'good parent' and it may not work. You might fumble. Your child might rebel. You might lose your cool.

If this happens, you might feel like there's something wrong with you. If this is your experience, pause. Reflect. Recognise that some people who are practising this stuff well might have come with fewer children. Or less emotional and psychological baggage. Or perhaps they have a more supportive partner or family. Maybe they have a firmer financial foundation, so they don't carry the same stress and burden you carry. It could be that they were raised in a need-supportive environment and so this is all second nature to them. Perhaps they've paid for endless amounts of coaching or therapy. Or done a PhD on the topic!

If the unintended consequence of reading a book like this is that you feel lousy, acknowledge that there are countless other people struggling in precisely the same way. Everyone struggles, fails, and experiences opportunities for new learning. This elegant, need-supportive solution may not be what you need right this minute (or perhaps it is what you need, but you're not quite ready for it). Don't – please, don't – feel ashamed or incompetent or incapable or in any other way insufficient if this is you. Instead, recognise that you're human. A parent who's carrying a lot. And that's okay.

Parenting is often about parenting yourself, not your child. It's a long-term process, but we too often measure the success of it by its short-term product (what our kids do). We can't ever really control the end product, and can only do our best in guiding it. So unless we were lucky enough to have 'easy' kids, we set ourselves up for failure from the start. We focus on our child's progress instead of our progress in our parenting and parenting skills.

But stick with it; the benefits are definitely worth it. In the next part of this book, there are practical tips to help you implement this approach, irrespective of your present circumstances.

Part 3:
Need-supportive parenting

This final section of the book will focus on our parenting and our parenting skills by looking at a range of tricky parenting challenges, some considering what need-supportive parenting *could* look like in each of these situations.

12 Making mornings magic

Mornings are consistently hard work for most families. There's too much to do and it seems like it's never done on time. We look at the clock and feel convinced we've got this, but then it's like wading through mud. The kids decide they're tired and unmotivated. Their legs hurt. They can't walk. They're feeling sick. Ugh! They'd rather be anywhere but school.

On reflection – and considering the basic psychological needs of our children – this makes sense. For too many children, school is a place where autonomy needs are frustrated rather than supported. Many children spend their days at school feeling incompetent. (Competence needs are fragile.) And a good number of children struggle with relationships at school, both with their teacher/s and their peers. Motivation is low when needs are frustrated, thwarted, or not supported.

How can need-supportive parenting help you get your kids happily off to school? Involvement, structure, and autonomy will be at the heart of the solution to this problem. What follows are some suggested steps, although not every step will work in every family.

Create a conversation

There are three things to remember before the conversations with your child start. First, your child really does want to do well. Dr Ross Greene, author of *The Explosive Child*, and the brain behind a parenting program called Collaborative and Proactive Solutions, reminds us that 'kids do well if they can'. Need-supportive parenting recognises an innate desire to figure things out and get things right. Second, if this is true, our job is to trust our child's developmental trajectory and acknowledge that things will work out. The third and final thing to remember is that we won't establish structures and expectations effectively without seeing the world through our child's frame of reference.

As for the conversation about getting to school on time: don't start conversations about a tricky topic while you're in the middle of dealing with the issue. Running late for school? Now's not the time to tell the kids to do better. Emotions are high. Intelligence is low. Communication will be poor. Solutions will be controlling, short-term, and ineffective. Instead, make a note that this issue will need to be discussed when everyone is calm and there's time for a conversation.

When you do have the conversation, set the scene so it's enjoyable by having a treat, a drink, or a walk together.

Spend some time being curious about the issue. Say to your child, 'Mornings have been pretty rough lately. We're late a lot, and we seem stressed out.' Ask questions like, 'Why do you think that is?' and 'What have you been noticing?'

At this stage it's not about chasing solutions. It's about exploration, understanding, and clarification of the issue.

Next, explain what you value. Keep it short. You might say something along these lines: 'I get that you like slow mornings and you don't like being at school that much. But I'm a bit stuck because school's compulsory, and I've got to be on time for work.'

Now empower your child to develop a solution with you. This guided empowerment sounds like, 'What do you think we can do to make mornings work better?' or 'If we could do one or two things differently to feel better in the morning, what would they be?' The purpose of this final element in the discussion is to develop the structures (expectations and limits) to facilitate effective morning routines, and improve the getting-ready-for-the-day experience.

What the reality could look like

Need-supportive parenting increases involvement, sets up structures, and amplifies autonomy. From Chapter 7, we know that need-supportive parenting is characterised by:

1 encouraging choice and initiative by carefully guiding children through problem-solving and collaborative limit-setting

2 providing a clear rationale and explanation for behavioural requests when made

3 recognising the feelings and perspectives of the child

If a conversation like this occurred, your child might acknowledge that mornings are a mess, and put forward ideas such as: better organisation is useful, music is fun, parents are too bossy, kids need a checklist, and hot chocolate and smoothies are the best incentive for getting out of bed. This input moves us towards solutions. Together, problems can now be solved. Structures can be developed in a child-led situation where possible. They're agreed to, and they're implemented. Your conversation might also uncover bigger issues like academic difficulties that are leaving children feeling incompetent and not wanting to be at school. Perhaps there are social challenges with your child struggling in friendships or being bullied. By discussing challenges in a need-supportive way, you create a foundation for progress. Pushing your children out the door without understanding undermines this process.

Assuming no major difficulties, getting things to work better for your mornings is still a big topic. A lot of families have grappled with it, so why not look at their ideas too. Most seem to find that preparation is key. Hint: your morning begins the night before.

Here are some of these other ideas – I've bundled them together in a slightly over-the-top way to make it fun and to emphasise options. Consider with your child what might work for your family and rein it in accordingly.

Imagine that after dinner each evening, the kids fill in a checklist for the next morning. They write down what they'll eat for breakfast. Perhaps a list of options might be on a pre-printed piece of paper, just like the menu in a hotel or restaurant: yogurt, eggs (poached, scrambled, fried, or omelette), cereal, spaghetti or baked beans, toast, fruit juice, smoothie. They simply tick the box and tomorrow's decisions are made. Then they make a plan for what they'd like to eat for lunch. Again, options could be listed for selection on a laminated menu; for example, leftovers, sandwiches, wraps, or whatever other creative options you can develop together. As parents, it's on you to ensure you have the right food available in the fridge. Mornings without milk and bread don't work, so shopping is one of your responsibilities. With food decisions made the night before, things should be more efficient in the morning.

Because your morning begins the night before, put structures in place like making sure, every night, that uniforms are ironed, shoes and socks are where they need to be, hats are sorted, and everything is set out for the next day, including school bags and lunchboxes. If it's sports day or library day, everything is laid out and prepared. We don't want to be searching the house for anything in the morning rush, so it all needs to be organised before bed.

And finally, a reasonable bedtime is important. Decisions about where screens will be kept might be made. This simple structural shift could have a lot of positive knock-on effects.

Next, you might agree that it would help to:

- Create a checklist with your children where *they* identify what is required each morning. If you're constantly telling the kids what to do in the mornings, this will save you energy. Stick it on their wall. Use pictures if they're too young to read. And no rewards. That's the shallow end of the motivation continuum. Just a check-box if they want to tick that they've done it.

- Wake up 10 minutes early. Start the day off by getting up earlier than you need to – and by getting the kids up earlier than they need to. But do it gently and kindly. Sit on your kids' beds and scratch their backs. Spend a few minutes talking to them about their day and what they're looking forward to. Then let them know it's time to get moving and you're there to help if they need it.

- Offer to help, but don't do it all. Working through a process like this means that your children will likely have a higher level of motivation for the morning. Enjoy watching your kids do their stuff. They'll leave their room dressed for school because, guess what? Their clothes were laid out the night before. They'll walk into the kitchen, grab their food list, and organise things themselves because it was laid out the night before. Your role- is to be benignly involved, support the structure, and encourage autonomy. If they're stuck, ask 'how can I help?' and let them guide.

Sounds too good to be true?

Now and then you'll still have one of those mornings where nothing works. But this tends to be the result of a late night, a lack of preparation the night before, or our failure to ensure that there's all the right food! Other issues will arise from time to time. A child who had a fight with a friend one day may not want to go to school the next morning. There may be some sibling rivalry over who gets to use the toaster or the bathroom first. But so long as we're on top of the things we can control, no one fights over the last yogurt cup.

It's true that this process requires time and attention in the evenings, which is tough if parents work late. And it's true that some of these tasks are a challenge for kids under five – but you can adapt the method and delegate tasks that your child is up to. Maybe a preschooler wants to butter her own toast or slice a banana.

These suggested structures may not work for you. Your children may be at different ages or have different needs. Perhaps you're on your own or juggling shiftwork. What matters here isn't the specific strategies (and the ones I've outlined are merely suggestions). What matters is the process of involving yourself with your kids, developing structures and boundaries/expectations, and encouraging autonomy and choiceful action.

Mornings are busy, but they don't have to be tough. A need-supportive parenting approach can smooth the way. It won't make it perfect. Adjustments will be necessary on a consistent basis. But a process like this really can help you make mornings magic, because it supports competence, relatedness, and autonomy needs through structure, involvement, and autonomy support.

13 School refusal

A natural follow-on to our last chapter is to recognise that sometimes mornings are awful because a child doesn't want to be at school. There is some evidence that Covid pandemic restrictions exacerbated this challenge.[1] If we acknowledge the importance of seeing the world through our child's frame of reference and slow down enough to take their perspective, it makes an enormous difference. This is a hallmark of need-supportive parenting. Let me repeat again, the essential elements that allow us to be involved, create structure, and facilitate autonomy.

Need- supportive parenting is characterised by:

1 Encouraging choice and initiative by carefully guiding children through problem-solving and collaborative limit-setting

2 Providing a clear rationale and explanation for behavioural requests when made

3 Recognising the feelings and perspectives of your child

With these points in mind, let's step into a messy morning of school refusal.

School refusal from a parent's perspective

You're glancing at the clock every 90 seconds. The space between making it and not making it is closing. 'Hurry up!'

Initially it's a polite reminder. 'We need to be on time today. Let's get things moving, okay sweetheart?' But as your child continues to stall, your tone shifts. Urgency creeps in. Then fear; you don't want to be late. Not today. Then frustration. Now you're at boiling point. Paradoxically, the more force you apply, the more your child resists. 'I don't want to go to school. I'm not going. You can't make me. It's not fair.'

You never wanted to be this kind of parent. You're feeling like an ogre. But being out the door on time is a priority. It matters. You can't be late. It's happened too often. You feel desperate. Helpless. Angry. And so sad for this child who you love so much, because the fact that they don't want to go to school means things aren't quite right for them somewhere, somehow. You just don't know what to do, but you don't have time to figure it out because that clock is still ticking, the space is still shrinking, and your child still won't put on their school uniform and help you get out the door on time.

What is school refusal?

School refusal is one of the most common challenges parents bring to me as they search for answers to make their mornings run smoother and their families function better. A child who's unwilling to get organised and out the door for school is generally a major impediment to the efficient running of the home.

Firstly, if a child doesn't want to go to school, perhaps we can dig a little deeper into why. Maybe there's bullying or some other situation to explore. As I've already said a couple of times in this book, school can be terribly challenging for children for a host of reasons. It may be one of the most unnatural things we ask of our children in our fast-paced, modern society. When a child doesn't want to do something, rather than forcing them to do it, it's useful to pause and consider the value of what we're asking of them in the first place.

In recent times there's been a movement to rename school refusal, and with good reason. To suggest a child is refusing school is to suggest that there's something 'wrong' with the child, or that the child needs an attitude adjustment and after that everything will be fine.

A more appropriate term is 'emotion-based school avoidance'. Others call it 'school can't'. In this chapter I'll use the term 'school refusal' since it's the one most familiar to most parents, but I do so with sensitivity, acknowledging that if your child is refusing to attend school, their avoidant behaviour is often justified and understandable.

Unfortunately, there's little research to guide our discussion. That's because it's staggeringly hard to research school refusal. The challenge is that a child might refuse to go to school for a day or two, then be okay. Consequently the parents don't seek help ... but then it happens again here and there, slowly building over the term until at least 10 days have been lost – or dozens of 'tardies' have been logged – and the problem is embedded. Help might be sought then, but by this point it's a much more difficult problem to work through than it might have been early in the piece. And there are few, if any, simple solutions. (We'll talk about why that is, and what solutions might be helpful shortly.)

One thing we do know, however, is that the incidence of school refusal is on the rise. Since Covid-19 lockdowns, there has been a measurable increase.[96]

What school refusal looks like

If your child is engaging in school refusal then you've likely experienced these typical difficulties:

- verbal refusal

- emotional outbursts when being prompted to prepare for school

- complete unwillingness to dress for school, pack lunch or a schoolbag, or leave the house

- tantrums

- panic attacks

- emotional explosions

- aggression

- tears

School refusal usually ends in power struggles, tantrums from both child and adult, and forceful efforts to get the child dressed, fed, in the car, through the school gate, and into the classroom. Ironically, by far the majority of parents tell me that, once they get their child to school, the teacher will report back later in the day, 'They're fine.' (This is definitely not the case for all children, but it does happen with surprising frequency, especially when children are young.)

But an important note on this: children (particularly girls) are very good at appearing fine. They can pull it together for the sake of saving face, but it doesn't mean that the anxiety isn't swirling like a whirlpool underneath.

Problematic absenteeism

If your child:

- misses at least two weeks of school in a single school term (without a legitimate reason such as illness), or

- has such difficulty attending school that it significantly interferes with daily life for at least two weeks

this would be categorised not as school refusal but as problematic absenteeism.

In both school refusal and problematic absenteeism, severe antisocial tendencies are rare. Your child will be angry and upset. She'll be saying 'no' and doing all she can to delay or avoid going to school. But it won't typically include significant aggression and violence, breaking things, swearing, and other antisocial acts. If these things are occurring, seek additional help.

Is there a diagnosis?

There are no clinical criteria for school refusal, but many school refusers meet criteria for specific phobias, generalised anxiety, social anxiety, separation anxiety, or depressive symptoms. If your child is refusing to attend school in an ongoing manner, you may find visiting your mental health care provider helpful.

Your child's perspective

One of the vital elements of need-supportive parenting is to see the world through your child's eyes. So let's try that. Why are so many children refusing to go to school? There are many difficult-to-solve reasons. Some relate to our children's relationships at school. The school environment is also implicated in a lot of school refusal, as it tends to frustrate and thwart our children's basic psychological needs (of relatedness, competence, and autonomy). Family context and parent factors can play a part too.

Let's take a look at some more common and significant reasons for school refusal:

- Feelings of disconnection

- Negative peer experiences

- Bullying and social isolation/ostracism

- Poor student–teacher relationships

- A low sense of school belonging

- Academic pressure

- Learning difficulties or disorders (including dyslexia, colour blindness, or speech/language challenges)

- Additional needs (such as ASD, ADHD, sensory issues, and more)

- Abuse or neglect

- Parental anxiety, depression, anger, or stress

- Parental overinvolvement (helicoptering)

- Poor family functioning

- Child anxiety or other mental health challenges

These are the big things that lead to school refusal challenges and, potentially, to problematic absenteeism. But basic (and typically less problematic) school refusal can be due to simple things like:

- A lousy night's sleep

- Feeling crappy that day (we're all allowed to have bad days, aren't we?)

- A fight with a sibling

- Homework or an assignment not complete and fear of detention

- Not being invited to a birthday party that everyone else was invited to

- Someone making a threat on the way home from school the day before

- A substitute teacher coming in that day

- School activities (like PE) that create a high level of self-consciousness

It can feel like we need to be mindreaders to work out why our kids don't want to go to school. And then we've got to work out what to do about it!

Yet something does need to be done. Cautiously. Sensitively. Compassionately. But definitely. That's because, once school refusal is established, it's more difficult to treat than it is when there are some minimal signs it's there. Being aware and acting will make a difference.

Cognitive and developmental realities

Our children are wired – literally biologically designed – to be close to us, to stay near those they love and trust, and to connect with people who make them feel safe. Sending them to school can undermine those feelings of security and safety. It can interfere with their sense that the world is predictable. To many children, notably those who are neurodiverse and living with additional needs, school feels random, volatile, unpredictable, and far too big. It also feels isolating and disconnecting as a result of a lack of quality relationships.

School refusal invariably shows up with big emotions: high in energy and high in unpleasantness. So what are we to do? How do we navigate school refusal, particularly in the early stages before we might typically seek outside help?

School refusal solutions

The solutions I offer below are varied and in no special order. Some might prove to be magic. Others may spell disaster. And the thing is, you really can't tell what will work and what won't. Something might work one day and flop the next. Other things might be perfect time after time after time. But remember the need-supportive elements that will help you find suitable solutions.

Explore the challenge with your child. Trying to talk about school refusal while things are awful isn't going to help. But on the weekend or during the holidays, perhaps you can explore what's happening in relation to school in a less confrontational way. Timing matters here.

Understanding rather than reprimanding; exploring rather than exploding. These compassionate conversations help you to see the world through your child's eyes and understand the challenge for them. After exploring, you might explain what you see as the issue. And again, empower your child to find a solution they feel fine about so they can act in a choiceful way moving forward. It will likely be a slow process. It could be better if an aunt or grandparent has the conversation. What matters is that the conversation takes place.

Issues around school refusal are complex, and it's possible that a conversation will only trigger explosive outcomes. Maybe the situation is so dire that any conversation reinforces the problem, undermines feelings of safety and security, and pushes your child further away from healthy, functional decisions. Use your parental wisdom and discernment.

Understand your child's needs. Children tend to have higher intrinsic motivation when three things come together:

- Their relationships are good

- They feel like they're mastering their environment

- They sense their life is under control

Your child will be likely to say 'no' to school if relationships are lousy (or non-existent), they're struggling academically, or they feel like they lack control and autonomy. If more than one of these things is occurring, the negative effects will be amplified. Most children struggle with some of these things at some point or other ... but some children struggle with all of these things – often all at once. Neurodiverse children are most likely to experience these basic psychological needs not being met. But if we're to reduce the school refusal, meeting these needs must be foremost in our minds and actions.

Recognise, however, that the school environment is out of your control. Need-supportive parents are all about creating a need-supportive environment. You can do that at home. You can't do that at school. Therefore, there are other things that may be necessary so your child can feel as though school supports basic psychological needs as well as home does.

Talk with teachers

Teachers might hold the key to your child's worries in their hands. They're often aware of social or academic issues that might be causing difficulty. Work with the school to arrange supports. These might be a special 'before school assignment' designed to help your child ease into the school day. They could establish lunchtime activities, or offer reduced homework. If your child is struggling academically and doesn't want to attend school because of learning difficulties, a tutor may be a useful consideration. A child who feels competent is more likely to develop confidence.

Make your mornings magic

Assuming your family has determined that school attendance will remain the expectation, the way you start your days can offset a negative emotion. A calm morning routine can be the difference between a child happily going to school and a child refusing to go to school at all. In the previous chapter I outlined the importance of preparing the night before, waking up a little earlier than needed, having a clear routine and system, and keeping things calm while building up your child's capacity and competence when getting ready for the day.

Build up friendships

When your child is looking forward to being with someone at school, it's less likely that school refusal will play a part in your morning. Find creative ways to help your child develop and strengthen relationships. Perhaps a sleepover, a movie afternoon on the weekend, some extracurricular activities, a joint family picnic at the park, or even a text to a few parents to see if they'll meet somewhere with the kids one afternoon or weekend. These activities draw children together (when done well) and help your child consolidate relationships.

Expand your view of what the problem may be

Any number of things could be a cause or contributor. And any number of things might be your solution. Be open to possibilities and solutions. You might find distraction is helpful. Or using the timer to keep forward momentum. Perhaps you'll find working together is the best way forward. Maybe it's meditation or mindfulness, more sleep, or a heartier breakfast. Maybe Mum is triggering for your child but Dad's approach seems to work. It could be that a change of schools is needed – a place with more friends, or a fresh start? And it may be none of those things. But be open. Try things out. Exercise hope. Be resourceful. Engage with your child. And recognise that your child may not actually have a clue why they don't want to be at school, and why everything is so hard. Medical issues, psychological challenges, or some other mystery might be at the heart of the matter. Who knows? A patient approach is vital.

Seek medical guidance

The reasons your child isn't eager to attend school might be hard to detect. Perhaps you're dealing with undiagnosed dyslexia, ADHD, autism, anxiety, or another medical, psychological, or neurological condition. For established, longer-term school refusal, working with a multidisciplinary mental health team may be required.

Change schools

Sometimes the best thing we can do is change schools. Send your child to a new place with people they don't know to give them a fresh start. (New starts can be extremely tough though, so be discerning with this solution.)

Alternative school solutions – private and state-funded – should be on your radar as potential strategies here too. Perhaps distance education might be the circuit-breaker you need, even for a short time. Maybe it's home school.

Is traditional school right for your child?

This may be the most fundamental question of all. School can put a lot of pressure on children. They've got to find a friendship circle, navigate classes, sports, and other activities, deal with different attitudes and expectations from adults around them (including people who aren't consistently in their lives), learn and retain substantial quantities of new information, manage being away from loved ones for large parts of the day, and so much more.

Yes

Most children adjust to school without too much fuss. But the mainstream school system doesn't suit everyone. For a variety of reasons, attending a conventional school might not be the best option for your child. And research supports the benefits that those children can find when effective alternative arrangements are made.

There's good evidence that most parents who decide to home-educate in response to school refusal report that their children's physical and psychological symptoms lessen or disappear. They behave better. Their anxiety drops. And many families choose to continue with home-educating as a result. But be aware that, typically, children require a period of 'de-schooling' before improvements are fully realised.

Before making a choice like this, here are practical realities parents must consider. Even if it's better for your child, can you afford it? Are you willing to put the considerable time and energy required into educating your child yourself? What resources can you access to encourage your child to develop friendships outside the home setting? How will you transition your child into their life after home-schooling is done? But from my perspective, home-schooling should be considered as an option for many children refusing school.

Some advice for all occasions

Ultimately, a child who exhibits school refusal behaviours is going to become emotionally elevated as we attempt to prod them towards the school gates. We can best support our children by improving emotional regulation. How? These steps can guide the conversation you have with your child as you explore their challenge, explain your preferences, and empower them to find solutions and implement structures with your guidance.

- Stay calm and see your child's emotions as a chance to connect, not correct.

- Describe the emotions you're seeing in your child (name it to tame it).

- Allow the emotion to occur in a safe way and a safe place (without trying to fix it).

- When things are calm, problem-solve and find solutions and limits together.

Avoidance reinforces anxiety

Sometimes you might do everything I've outlined and still find yourself at a 7.55 am impasse. You've started the car. You've honked the horn. You're running late and the pressure is rising. In this instance there are no easy answers. But I offer a caution: avoidance reinforces anxiety.

When your child discovers that refusal and tantrums lead to permission to avoid school, it feels wonderful to them, at least initially. But over time it changes, and begins to feel horrible. Your child can feel like a failure. She feels unworthy and stupid and pathetic. But, frustratingly, to her it's still better to feel like that than to have to face school.) The reprieve feels rewarding enough that it provides reinforcement to the idea that school is better when it's avoided, and this can become a cue. In other words, tomorrow at breakfast time the anxieties return, and recalling that feeling of relief from the day before cues a craving to remain at home. In response, the craving kicks off challenging behaviours. And we find ourselves in the same tense stand-off over and over again, culminating in the reward of staying out of school, reinforcing the cue that kicked it off in the first place.

I say this cautiously: if you can get your child to school without excessive outrage, and if your child seems to settle into school, it may be worth pushing through the challenges. But it really is an individual thing. Proceed carefully, compassionately, and where possible, collaboratively.

A personal experience

If we consider the process a conversation might take as we navigate school refusal with our children, a personal experience might be useful here.

One of my children has found school awful for much of her schooling life. She has high academic expectations of herself and achieves well at school. However, some of her basic psychological needs are thwarted in the school environment and she resists being at school. Some additional personal challenges add to the difficulties she has with school.

One morning as we prepared to leave for school we became aware that she wasn't dressed or packed. We asked what was going on and the reply was clear: 'I'm not going.'

After taking a moment to recalibrate, I sat with my daughter and spent a long time listening as we explored her school worries and troubles. These were serious issues for her. Eventually she was all talked out. I asked if I might make some observations, and with her consent I explained what I understood she'd told me. She clarified a few things and then confirmed that I really did understand. Check! I could see things from her frame of reference.

I asked if she understood why school attendance mattered. She understood the rationale for why we were asking her to attend school. (This should not take more than a few moments. Kids get bored when we lecture.)

Lastly, once expectations were understood, I asked her how we could work this out. Because she was emotional, all I received was a shoulder shrug. Then tears. We hugged, and I asked more questions to understand her situation even more. As she spoke, my daughter said something striking: 'I hate Tuesday and I hate Friday.' 'Why?' I queried. Her explanation led to an idea: 'How about we organise for you to have Fridays off for the rest of term? You work from home. You do the required work, but you don't do it there. You do it here. Can you handle four days instead of five? Would that work?'

A smile lit up her face as she asked, in wonder, 'Can we really do that?' And a solution that felt choiceful and positive for my daughter led to a shift in the way she felt about school.

Is this the solution for everyone? Not at all! Is it even close to an optimal solution for most people? Potentially not.

The solution here isn't the point of sharing this episode. The process is what matters. Careful, compassionate, focused listening to explore. Concise, clear explanations to establish anticipated structure.

Collaborative, considered guidance as we empower and encourage our children to find solutions or step into solutions we suggest. Relatedness, competence and autonomy needs are being supported.

School refusal is a sign that something is wrong – and that something is *not* your child. It might be an issue with the school environment. It could be an issue with home life. It may even be a sign that your child is struggling with some big challenges themselves. If school refusal is occurring, a need-supportive parenting process is at the heart of moving through the challenges you face. Additionally, bringing a care team on board can increase chances of successfully seeing your child resume school attendance. Talk to a GP about setting up a mental health care plan, talk to the school principal or school wellbeing team, recruit friends (yours and your child's), plan gatherings, and build resources for your child's wellbeing.

Most practitioners stress the desirability of a swift return to school. The consequences of missing school quickly snowball (for instance, it's hard to catch up – and to graduate – after falling behind academically for long stretches) because those needs of relationships and mastery are undermined and school becomes increasingly threatening.

The take-home message is all about need support: listen to your child. Really understand their needs. Build connection. And be patient. Being a parent is one of the hardest jobs there is. The only one that's almost certainly harder is growing up.

14

How do I get my kids to do their homework?

In 2014, the Victorian State Government launched an inquiry into homework in the state's schools. Its findings were equivocal. Proponents of homework argued that its benefits included:

- improving understanding of classwork

- getting good grades

- opportunities to practise skills

- preparation for the next lesson

- help in developing good discipline

- independent learning skills

- developing time management and study skills

Nevertheless, thin evidence was provided to support these ideas, particularly in relation to the last four items on the list. Further – and of critical importance – the inquiry summary states that:

The case against homework is based not on evidence
of its negative effects, but on the perceived absence of
evidence that it actually aids learning. By this argument,
if there are no clear benefits, then the potential damage
it can do in adding to pressure on young people already
under developmental stress, taking young people away
from family and other relationships, impinging on time
for extracurricular activities that have health and social
benefits and in widening the gap between advantaged
and disadvantaged students, makes homework not
worth doing. It is also argued that the role of 'homework
policing' by parents creates tensions in the family that
arise because of the resentment of children, particularly in
adolescence, of further loss of autonomy.[1]

The inquiry also acknowledged that there's a noticeable lack
of evidence that homework is a benefit to primary-school-aged
children. It seems that whatever benefits homework does offer, they
don't appear in research data until high school.

Alfie Kohn, whose books include *The Homework Myth*, makes
strident arguments against homework for younger children.
He presents global research that underscores the findings of the
parliamentary committee's inquiry. And yet the school system
requires that teachers continue to give homework, and many
parents push for more without understanding the lack of evidence
to support its use.

Over the years I've sat in many parent–teacher evening talks
at the commencement of the school year. Often primary school

teachers have suggested they have low homework expectations, only to be met with fiery responses from well-intentioned parents who truly believe their child 'won't keep up' (or get ahead) unless homework is set every night.

Question the value before you question your child

A principle of need-supportive parenting that applies equally to homework and every other pain point we experience with our children is that of recognising the importance of asking *why something matters* before making demands of our children to do that thing. In a podcast interview, Alfie Kohn told me:

> If a child is ... rolling the eyes because frankly, we're saying stuff that deserves an eye roll, then the problem is not the kid. The problem is with what we have been doing; that we have to rethink ... In other words the premise of the question ought to be called into question. Don't ask 'How do I get the kid to do x if I can't use punishments and rewards?' Begin by asking whether x really needs to be done. But if we're convinced it does ... then I would be asking the child, 'What's the problem here? What can be done? What do you think you can do in order to help things go smoothly?' Kids learn to make good decisions by making decisions, not by following directions.

When it comes to homework, the need for our primary-school-aged children to be doing it is a hard argument to make. There's a lack of evidence supporting it, it interferes with family time and extracurricular activities, it places stress on our kids and on us (because who really knows how to help with homework once the children have reached Grade 4), and it often creates conflict. Therefore, I don't encourage homework at all in primary school. Some kids want to do it. That's fine. Don't stop them. And if your child is staring at a screen all afternoon and evening, then perhaps the homework will be a useful activity to move them away from idleness. But my general position, based on current evidence, is that homework is best avoided in favour of a full and active extracurricular life outside school with plenty of unstructured time and a few structured activities. For high school children, homework is useful and is to be encouraged (up to 2 hours per night in senior years).

In spite of my misgivings with homework, however, there are two things that must be addressed in this chapter in relation to education:

1 The value and importance of reading (at all ages)

2 The challenges of homework – and motivation for schoolwork more generally – for our older children

Reading and motivation

It's a superpower that's available to all: reading – alone, out loud, or with someone – is associated with strong and positive educational outcomes. The list of advantages that children who are highly literate experience educationally, socially, psychologically, cognitively, and emotionally is substantial. Reading matters. But reading is not homework. Reading is for joy! If reading is joyful, you won't have a hard time encouraging your children to read. Regrettably, parents and teachers often turn reading into a chore. How?

Many children are asked to complete a 'reading wheel' or other tracker, designed to ensure a minimum amount of time is spent on a book. What does this do to basic psychological needs? Time limits leave children watching the clock more than the words on the page. Minimum page quotas lead them to the easiest books with the fewest words. This removal of autonomy turns reading into a horrible task that 'must' be done, rather than a pleasure. The other challenge is that many books children are asked to read are boring. Even if they're good books, sometimes a child will be uninterested because the book isn't appealing to them.

While homework is not great for kids, reading is amazing for them. If your child is not motivated to read, the solution, as in previous chapters, is need-supportive parenting. And the elements do not change from those we've reviewed a number of times now.

Explore why your child isn't reading. Spend time being involved with books and your child by reading with them and having them read to you. This will build competence. To support autonomy, let them choose the books they're interested in, even if they don't do much for you! (As a quick aside, I promise you that of the countless books my daughters and I have read together over the years, few have been riveting for me. But that's beside the point. They've been interested in them. And that's all that matters.)

The best way to make children hate reading is to make them prove to us or others that they have read. The next best way to discourage children from reading is the use of rewards for completing a book – such as stars, goodies, etc. If they read a book and receive a chocolate or some cash as a prize – or pizza, as some American schools have trialled – the book isn't motivating for the child. The prize is. That type of reward will undermine intrinsic motivation over time. However, one thing that's highly motivating is to let your children know that, when they've completed one book, you'll gladly get them another one immediately, either from the bookstore (at a price) or the library (at no cost). If it's motivating to read one book, it's doubly motivating to be able to read another one. The 'motivator' here may be partly extrinsic, but it reinforces the intrinsic delight found in reading.

Big kids and schoolwork

It's one thing to deal with homework and reading challenges with young children. But what about bigger kids? The process of engaging with teenagers on anything they have a fixed attitude towards can be daunting.

Let's unpack this topic carefully and start by reminding ourselves about the key message. I've reiterated this in every chapter (because repetition is how we learn).

Need-supportive parenting is characterised by:

1 encouraging choice and initiative by carefully guiding children through problem-solving and collaborative limit-setting

2 providing a clear rationale and explanation for behavioural requests when made

3 recognising the feelings and perspectives of your child

With older children, a need-supportive parent will start with the third element. For many of our children, school is torture. It feels like a prison – a place they're trapped while being force-fed facts that feel irrelevant to their lives. Children who don't engage with learning at school are often dealing with additional needs, social difficulties, learning challenges (that may be undiagnosed), or motivational frustrations!

The second thing need-supportive parents do is pause and acknowledge that their child will be drawn towards growth and development opportunities (that is, they'll be motivated) when the environment is supportive of their needs. We have to trust in that intrinsic quest for growth inside each of our children, even when we cannot see it. Quality relationships, learning opportunities that are choiceful, and that are building competence by being situated on the edge of their current ability: these environmental elements will support identified, integrated, and even intrinsic motivation in our children. Is this the school environment your child experiences?

We have options when dealing with a teen who feels that school, homework, and study are tedious. A conversation with a teacher may help. For those with sufficient resources, a school that actively supports their child's needs will be better than one that doesn't. (The last chapter briefly described pros and cons of school change.) But more often than not, we go back to the conversations that are at the heart of all of our problem-solving situations with our kids. We explore their world with compassion. We explain our expectations and preferences with clarity. And then we empower our child to discover solutions to the challenge we're facing collaboratively.

Let's consider a couple of quick examples.

Your high schooler is refusing to do homework, preferring to game, use social media, sleep, hang out, do nothing.

1. When you're both calm and rational and not in the moment (remember, high emotions = low intelligence), ask if you can chat about a problem you're struggling with.

2. Describe what you're observing – without mean names, horrifying predictions about their future, or anything else overly emotional. Perhaps you could say, 'I'm feeling nervous about how you're doing with your schoolwork and wanted to talk about it together.'

3. Ask for their input. 'How are you feeling about school generally?' Really try to understand what's happening for them, and withhold judgment, scare tactics, or fixes.

4. Invite them to tell you why they think you're nervous. This is powerful because it shows you whether they really understand your issue.

5. Pause and restate it all. 'So you're frustrated and bored. And you're struggling with Mr Browning? And I'm stressing out because I want you to do well.' Check in to see if there's anything else.

6 Finally, problem-solve. 'What do you think we can do to help you feel better about school, and help me feel better about how things are going?'

It's important to recognise that, in response to the above question, your child might shrug his shoulders and say 'nothing'. When motivation is low and other options are more appealing, kids sometimes prefer to ignore our concerns and ask us to leave them alone. And screens are more fun than schoolwork!

When this happens, let them know, 'We need to figure something out. But I get where you're coming from. It's really hard.' Then set an appointment. 'Let's puzzle this out some more on the weekend. No pressure from me just now. But it would be great if we can find some kind of a resolution.' Follow up on the weekend. And if your child still has nothing, offer to make some suggestions: 'I've had a couple of ideas. Are you open to hearing them?' And with their consent (which they'll give 99.9 per cent of the time if you've been need supportive), share some ideas and generate a conversation. Your emphasis will be on developing some structure to support your child's engagement with school.

Please recall Alfie Kohn's comment, however, that it's unfair to expect a child to be highly motivated to do something that holds limited intrinsic value.

These discussions don't always happen quickly. Solutions aren't always neat and tidy. That's family life! But this approach is more likely to be productive than a controlling, restrictive approach, and far more effective than a hands-off, permissive approach.

My child is throwing away their education

One major challenge many parents face is a senior student who's choosing not to work hard, and may not achieve a university entrance rank that's high enough to enrol in a course that's meaningful, either to the child or the parent. I'll share a personal story about the need-supportive way we've approached this issue in our own home. As I write this book, my third daughter has just completed her final year of high school. We've been here multiple times.

As Grade 11 begins, my wife and I sit with our child and affirm our support and delight in her. We explain that school is almost done, and we ask what her hopes and aspirations are. We then assure her we'll do all we can to support her in what she seeks, but we won't be responsible for her school attendance, study, or results. Those things, we gently indicate, are on her.

Next, we ask what we can do to help. Would she like tutoring? Changes to her study space? Regular reminders from us to do things? Peace, quiet, and autonomy? Pocket money rather than a job? (In our family we've always encouraged our children to have jobs.) We play with ideas and solve problems, letting our daughter take the lead. Through warm engagement and involvement, we establish structures together that are volitionally determined by her. And we reassure her that if things change, all she has to do is let us know.

A need-supportive process facilitates conversations about expectations in ways that preserve the relationship and elevate autonomy. It demonstrates that we believe in our child's competence, and allows us to develop structures that will be supportive. It enables our children to find joy in their final years of school, feel autonomous and choiceful, and focus on their personal goals rather than ours.

A last word on this. Not every child needs to go to university or should go to university. Only around 30 per cent of Australian adults have university degrees, and the majority without tertiary qualifications contribute significantly to society and provide well for their families. (You might argue that they contribute more, in case after case, than some with degrees.) Allowing your child autonomy to follow their energy and interests is a pathway to what will generally be a life well lived. And it will take the pressure off you and your family.

Once again we see this need-supportive process replicated. Become involved by exploring their world to meet their relatedness need. Trust in their innate growth tendencies and desire for mastery to support their competence need. And solve problems together to support their autonomy needs.

Remember – your dreams for your child are *yours*. Our job is not to raise a child who satisfies all of our hopes and dreams. It's to raise a child who can pursue and fulfil *their* hopes and dreams. And if they shrug their shoulders and say they don't have any dreams for the future, that's ok for now. The process stays the same. We patiently encourage them to persist in working hard so they have options when they *do* discover what path they wish to follow. And we gently but clearly work with them to find a pathway forward that is productive and positive.

15

How do I manage screens and kids?

Rick Riordan's novel *Percy Jackson and the Lightning Thief* became a bestselling book for tweens and teens in 2010. In the story, Percy and his friends, Annabeth and Grover, are on a mission to save the world. Racing across the USA, they're travelling through Las Vegas when, exhausted, they stumble into the Lotus Hotel and Casino for some rest. They enter the lobby and discover a breathtaking gaming complex. Screens litter the landscape. Children are playing them, drawn in by their seductive powers.

Rather than recovering from their long adventure and preparing to carry on with that really important mission – you recall, they had to save the world – the trio become absorbed in the screens and games. Percy begins playing a game with a guy called Darrin. He's dressed a little weird and uses words like 'groovy'. Percy becomes wary of Darrin's strange ways and eventually asks Darrin what year it is. Darrin looks up, surprised, and says, '1975'. Percy starts asking everyone what year it is and discovers that the Lotus Hotel and Casino is a time vortex – a trap. Video games are the bait. In the movie (though not in the novel), as Percy makes this realisation, a security guard speaks into his wristwatch, warning the other guards, 'Percy Jackson is awake.' Percy forces Annabeth and Grover from their screen-induced stupor, saying, 'This place is a trap … Annabeth, there are people here from 1977. Kids who have never aged. You check in, and you stay forever.'

In the early–mid 1990s the internet became a 'thing'. While early adopters were using primitive versions of the internet prior to then, it was around 1994 that email addresses and internet bulletin boards began to proliferate. Classmates, a website that connected people with old school friends, hit the World Wide Web in December 1995. The first real social media site launched in May 1997. You almost certainly won't remember it: Six Degrees. Why not? While everyone was discovering the internet by this time, very few people were using it the way we do now. The site had a lot of members but didn't last. In 2002, Friendster was launched, followed by LinkedIn in 2003 (yes, it's really that old!), and by the end of that year the world's first major social platform, Myspace, captured our attention. Facebook kicked off in 2004 and eclipsed everyone a few years later, becoming the controversial, ubiquitous juggernaut we now know (although its popularity is declining at present).

Other major players have continued to pop up and influence us, including Bebo (2005), Instagram (2010), Snapchat (2012), TikTok (it's complicated), and so many more. In 2012, the iPhone became omnipresent and mobile internet connection enveloped the world. The rise of technology and its influence over our lives, the way it's captured so much of our attention, has been astonishing, and it affects parents and families in profound and challenging ways.

Regardless of the age of your children, it's almost certain that screen usage forms a substantial part of their day. If it doesn't, your child would probably like it to. The intentionally designed features of devices and apps persuasively pull at all of humanity with alluring promises of connection, entertainment, learning, freedom, and relaxation. (Netflix and chill, anyone?) These promises are thin and shallow. Nevertheless, they pull almost all of us in and they're exceptionally powerful to our children.

My own view of screens and screen use has evolved over the past years as more and more research has come to light. Ultimately, thanks to the work of people like Tristan Harris at the Centre for Humane Technology and Johann Hari (author of *Stolen Focus*), I've become convinced that the model that drives the way we use screens is corrupted and harmful to our motivation and wellbeing. This model demands that we place increasing amounts of attention on our screens. Social media platforms, games, news websites, and more rely on our enduring focus in order to make money. The more time we spend on the screen, staring at their product, the more their platform prospers.

In 2021, China (hardly a beacon of need support, but stay with me here) prohibited 'minors' from playing video games on school days and for more than an hour on weekend and holiday nights. This resulted in Chinese teenagers flooding various platforms (like Twitch and YouTube) where they could watch other people livestreaming their gameplay. China created an update to the ban, preventing children from watching livestreams after 10 pm. Why? According to the Chinese government, they're attempting to reduce addiction to gaming – which they refer to as 'spiritual opium' – because of concerns about how it harms mental health and academic study.

Banning is unlikely to lead to positive outcomes. (We don't have data on outcomes on this intervention.) But this is external motivation in the extreme: commanding people to behave a certain way sits at the shallowest end of the motivation continuum. The thinking behind the government's decision, however, makes sense in light of what people like Tristan Harris and Johann Hari are telling us.

William Siu, a former game developer and founder of Storm8, knows a bit about this. He's launched more than 50 mobile games; collectively they've been downloaded over one billion times. (They've also generated more than one billion dollars in sales.)

In a *New York Times* essay, Siu explained:

> I am very familiar with game addiction, as that's what I thought about every day for more than a decade. (We sold the company in 2020.) I hired product managers and engineers to track everything players did and analyze their behavior. Using the data we collected, we experimented with every feature of our games to see which versions allowed us to extract the most time and money from our players. For us, game addiction was by design: It meant success for our business.

After explaining some of the techniques developers use to keep a user's rapt attention, Siu adds one more compelling statement: 'That's the ultimate goal: to build habit-forming games that have players coming back every day. In other words, it takes away the decision-making. We wanted people to reach for their phones first thing in the morning and jump right into our games, just as they check their social media and emails.'[1]

The games and platforms our children are using are not benign. They're designed by the smartest people in the world – thousands of them – who are analysing our every click, swipe, and touch to allow them to extract more time and money from us. Note that Siu identifies that games were designed to follow the model of social media designers and even email design. Each time we touch our device we give them more information to keep us there. Addiction to the platform is by design. That's the model. As Percy Jackson pointed out, 'It's a trap ... you check in and you stay forever.'

Is it any wonder that our children want to be on their screens? What hope do they have of fighting this mammoth machine that meets their relatedness, competence and autonomy needs so perfectly?

There are some who argue that time on screens is simply a new form of play. They complain that overblown hysteria is making more of this issue than is warranted. Perhaps they're right. But when I consider the issue, I look at the potential upside and downside of the various decisions we could make here. The upside of more time on screens is relatively modest. Relatedness needs may be met, but it's usually – though not always – a thin, wispy version of what face-to-face involvement feels like. Competence needs may be met, but is playing that game better than everyone else really going to change your life? (Maybe if you're a pro-gamer?) As Cal Newport states in *Deep Work*, giving kids screens to maximise their computer savvy is like giving a kid a Tonka truck so he can understand how to be a mechanic.

The downside of excessive screen usage though? It's significant. High levels of screen use displace sleep, physical activity, time in relationships with others, schoolwork and other learning, having a job, exploring hobbies, art, music, and other enriching interests that help build relationships and competence, reduce mind-wandering time, and more. Each of these are associated with living a whole and balanced life. Each of them contributes to wellbeing. And each is overrun by the carefully and intentionally designed screens and platforms that our children access.

There's an additional downside to briefly mention, which is the issue of content. So much of what appears on our screens is coarse, explicit, and vulgar. Our children's social media feeds are full of videos with the coarsest of language, the most vulgar and explicit song lyrics, and a variety of activities that also fall into those categories. Pornography in its vilest forms is available at the click of a button, simply by ticking a box that says 'I am over the age of 18 years'. In Season 2 of *Parental Guidance* we addressed this topic specifically, showing that children are naturally curious and some will succumb to the temptation of viewing illicit and explicit content – content that research evidence shows can harm them by changing their beliefs about intimacy (and the sexual script they feel they should follow), and ultimately influencing their behaviours when they have the opportunity to be intimate with someone.

Most parents recognise that this type of content isn't healthy for their children. But they also struggle with how to have the conversation about screens with the kids. It's incredibly challenging because of how compelling screens are, and the fact that they're ubiquitous!

It's tempting to offer a knee-jerk response to the trigger of screen time. That's not going to be helpful though. The following suggestions are going to be useful for every parent discussing screens with their children. The conversation will be simplified for younger children. You can go deeper with older children. It's the same process whether they have additional needs, want to be gaming, or just love social media.

You might find that emotions get a little higher than usual with a conversation like this. When that occurs, stop the conversation and reschedule it for later when things are calm. (Sometimes this discussion can take a few weeks to finalise.) It bears repeating that high emotions tend to lower intelligence, reduce creativity in problem-solving, and harm relationships.

The consistent message of this book is that we see far better outcomes with need-supportive parenting. In each previous chapter I've emphasised that need-supportive parenting is characterised by:

1 encouraging choice and initiative by carefully guiding children through problem-solving and collaborative limit-setting

2 providing a clear rationale and explanation for behavioural requests when made

3 recognising the feelings and perspectives of your child

Accordingly, we sit with our child with a mindset that we want to understand their perspective, communicate why we have concerns, and help them develop structures that will be useful in determining positive expectations for how screens are used in the home from this point forward.

A real life example

When Snapchat launched, my eldest daughter begged to be allowed to download the app. Knowing what I knew about its dangers, I said 'No.' I wasn't interested in being need supportive. I was preoccupied, didn't like the platform, and had limited interest in engaging in a long exploration of the topic with my 13-year-old. She responded by saying, 'Dad, I've been to your seminars. You can't just say no to me. You're supposed to explore, explain, and empower!'

While not entirely true (because sometimes parents must say no), I realised that in this case, she was right. Reluctantly I sat with her and explored as she told me her perspective. 'All of my friends have it. I'm the only one who doesn't have it. And besides, they ignore me on Facebook Messenger.'

I listened carefully, and even picked up a notepad and pen to write down her comments so she knew her voice was heard. And then I explained in detail why I was opposed to her having Snapchat. We itemised my concerns on the notepad. My list was compelling. But it wasn't enough.

'All my friends are on Snapchat, Dad. You don't understand! They don't even reply to my messages on Facebook anymore!'

I continued to insist that she use Facebook Messenger. 'Tell them your dad says they have to talk to you on Facebook!' I impotently demanded, as if that was going to work. But her pleas to be on

Snapchat continued until, in frustration, she used a metaphor to get her point across.

'Dad, you telling me to use Facebook while my friends are on Snapchat is kind of like you telling me to play at the park while all of my friends are at the beach.'

It was a persuasive statement. But I had a quick reply. 'The beach is so dangerous though! There are rips and sweeps and currents. There are sharks and bluebottles. There are syringes in the sand. There's the sun that burns. And, well, there are perverts there too.'

Chanel met my gaze, thought for a brief moment, and responded, 'Dad, have you been to the park lately?'

I had to give it to her. The kid had me. Gosh parenting is exhausting!

At that point our conversation turned. I saw things from her point of view. It made sense. I didn't agree, necessarily, but I realised that the issue was deeper than I'd been willing to countenance at the start of our conversation.

Your children want to be on their screens for social media and gaming because that's where their friends are. That's where the action is. That's where the conversation for tomorrow at school begins. Without it, they're isolated. They're out of the loop.

We continued our discussion. The beach/park metaphor was dropped, but we collaborated on a solution that would offer autonomy, structure, and healthy involvement – and it worked. Rather than me describing the conversation as it occurred, let's pretend the metaphor carried on throughout our problem-solving process. Had the metaphor been continued through our conversation, it might have gone like this:

Me: I see your point. I don't like it. I have serious concerns about it. But it makes sense. How do you think you can go to the beach, metaphorically speaking, in a way that I can feel good about?

Chanel: What if I promise to swim between the flags, wear sunscreen, and promise to only hang out with my friends? And what if I also said you could swing by to check up on me whenever you needed to. Could I go to the beach then?

By working out what the issues are and talking through them collaboratively, we were able to determine a pathway forward for my daughter that felt good for both of us. Her need for connection and involvement was satisfied. Her engagement with me on determining appropriate structures and boundaries to keep her safe supported competence needs, and it all rested on the collaborative empowerment approach that supported autonomy for my daughter.

(In the next chapter we'll address what to do when there's no way forward that we can feel good about in spite of our best efforts at collaborative problem-solving.)

Many parents think that using expensive apps is an easier alternative to having hard conversations (regularly) about screens. In the same way that fencing the pool doesn't protect your child from water (because they'll end up at a beach, lake, river, or other body of water one day, and you can't fence the ocean), putting an app on devices to filter and monitor children's behaviour won't protect your child from online challenges. It can impede some online activity, but once they're at a friend's home, or at school, or anywhere except your house, they could find themselves in metaphorical deep water not knowing how to swim. They are safest when we support learning and mastery, collaborate regularly by talking early and often about issues that arise with screens (like too much time, content, and impacts on wellbeing), and finding amenable solutions together.

Furthering this argument, research emphasises that letting children manage their own media consumption – with our gentle guidance, scaffolding, and structure – is typically more effective than parental control settings offered by apps. In a study called 'Coco's Videos', researchers at the University of Washington, Seattle, designed a video-streaming app for preschoolers – with three different versions, designed to see how persuasive design elements affected children's use of the app.

In the neutral version, a large 'home' button is displayed after the child has watched the selected video, and that button leads children back to the beginning of the app's menu, where they can make a new playlist. The second version of the app is called the 'post-play' version. Here, a child views the same home button at the end of their viewing. This time, however, in the top right corner of the image there's a small screen embedded which automatically plays a recommended video. The child now faces a choice: either expand the window to full-screen and watch, or pause the newly playing video and go back to the home screen via the prompt taking up the majority of the screen. In the third version, the child is automatically locked out of the app once they've finished a video playlist, meaning no auto-play. After three minutes, the app resets and returns to the home screen, and a new video playlist could be created.

It will surprise no parent who's ever given a child a screen that the post-play version (the one that automatically plays another video) led to a significant reduction in 'children's autonomy and … self-regulation'. Children watched the screen longer, and parents were therefore more likely to intervene to ask their child to 'get off the screen'. This auto-play feature is used extensively and by default by platforms such as YouTube and Netflix, as well as Facebook, Instagram (reels), and TikTok. The version that locked children out didn't reduce screen time or the likelihood of parent intervention. That is – controls didn't make a difference in this experiment.[2]

The study's take-home message was that more controls aren't helpful. What would be helpful is if technology platforms would act ethically by stopping the creation and implementation of these strategies, such as auto-play, infinity scroll, hiding the time, and so on (and therefore shift their business model away from stealing our children's focus and attention – and ours). At least the problem wouldn't be so overwhelming.

The same researcher, Alexis Hiniker, conducted another study with preschoolers and parents. In this instance, parents were asked to be involved with their kids, develop expectations and boundaries (structures) together, and give their children a voice in how screen and other activities could work together. Then the researchers watched. The results were astonishing: with parental guidance and collaborative, autonomy-supportive involvement during the discussion phase, children put their screens down and moved on to their next activity without their parents having to intervene, and it happened that way 93 per cent of the time.

Is there an argument for some filters and protective mechanisms? Yes. But those mechanisms are best implemented in conjunction with a conversation where a child says, 'I think we should set up the software to kick me off after a certain amount of time or at a specific time of the night.' That way the child is developing the structure and utilising the software as a resource to help. This is a vastly different situation to one where a parent uses control in order to restrict a child's screen access without giving the child a voice.

16

When you have to say 'no'

Wouldn't it be fantastic if our conversations with our kids always worked out like they did in the previous chapter? Imagine if we knew how to always stay calm, be rational, and have a considered and collaborative conversation with a child who wants something that may not be in their best interest. Imagine if our children could know how to always stay calm, be rational, and have a considered and collaborative conversation with an adult whose ideas are different to their own, but through respectful dialogue were able to work things out. Wouldn't it be great if it always worked out like that?

The fact is, sometimes we have to step in and say no. The real world isn't neat and tidy. Children are generally (and developmentally appropriately) irrational and immature. These reasonable conversations are hard, if not impossible at times. We have to be on our 'A' game, which isn't always possible since there are so many demands pulling us away from creating that need-supportive environment. In this chapter, we consider two questions that parents struggle with when it comes to need-supportive parenting.

1 This need-supportive parenting style seems to require a lot of time and a lot of talking. Do I have to do this all the time?

2 What is a parent supposed to do when a child's asking for something that demands a 'no' response? Are we supposed to be autonomy supportive even when they want to do something unsafe or unhealthy, or just plain stupid?

Fast and slow parenting

Need-supportive parenting can't be reduced to a few words, some power assertion, and a quick result. It's not a fast parenting style. By contrast, traditional parenting styles have solutions that seem to be easier and faster than need-supportive parenting demands; yelling, threats, withdrawal of privileges, grounding, time-out, smacking, and more. I call these responses puffer-fish parenting. We make ourselves big and threatening to get what we want. While these responses give the impression that they're effective, research tells us they're not. They don't 'work'. Rather, they're simple and neat, and definitely fast.

But fast is slow. How is this slow? Simple: we have to keep doing it again and again. We don't get a consistent, lasting result.

Let's do a quick parenting assessment.

Do we:

Use threats as punishment with little justification?
☐ Always   ☐ Sometimes   ☐ Never

Give in to our child when she causes a commotion about something?

☐ Always ☐ Sometimes ☐ Never

Yell or shout when our child misbehaves?

☐ Always ☐ Sometimes ☐ Never

Find it difficult to discipline our child?

☐ Always ☐ Sometimes ☐ Never

Punish by taking privileges away from our child?

☐ Always ☐ Sometimes ☐ Never

Scold and criticise when our child's behaviour doesn't meet our expectations?

☐ Always ☐ Sometimes ☐ Never

Use physical punishment as a way of disciplining our child?

☐ Always ☐ Sometimes ☐ Never

Threaten our child with punishment more often than actually giving it?

☐ Always ☐ Sometimes ☐ Never

Punish by putting our child off somewhere alone with little if any explanation (time-out)?

☐ Always ☐ Sometimes ☐ Never

Grab our child when being disobedient?

☐ Always ☐ Sometimes ☐ Never

Explode in anger towards our child?

☐ Always ☐ Sometimes ☐ Never

Scold and criticise to make our child improve?

☐ Always   ☐ Sometimes   ☐ Never

Smack when our child is disobedient?

☐ Always   ☐ Sometimes   ☐ Never

Threaten punishments to our child but don't follow through?

☐ Always   ☐ Sometimes   ☐ Never

These approaches may feel fast and effective, but they end up taking more time because of the way they damage the foundations of trust in our relationship with our child. Each time we've ticked 'always' or 'sometimes', it shows we've undermined our influence by making our child's environment less, rather than more, need supportive. That's because our child doesn't learn to do the right thing for the right reasons. They only learn to do the right thing when we're around so that they can get the goody or avoid the punishment. Their internalisation and moral development is slow. They're forced to live at the shallow end of the motivation continuum. Their progress into a responsible, thoughtful, considerate, intrinsically motivated individual is slowed or even stopped when we go for 'quick fire', because we're focused on compliance via external motivators.

Fast is slow. And slow is fast.

Need-supporting parenting requires considerable effort in the early phases. It's about laying a solid foundation in the relationship – one of trust, compassion and emotional availability – and spending time in effortful dialogue, guidance and teaching, developing structures and tentatively exploring collaborative empowerment for autonomy. This stuff is slow, and it can be hard work. But as time goes on, it's required less and less. And soon enough, slow becomes fast. Children trust us, learn from us, come to us for guidance, and love to be with us.

Slow means that, when our child is challenging and struggling, we spend time with him. We speak quietly. We listen. We're patient. We consider his preference to wait until the ads, or until he loses a life in his game. When we have to hurry, we talk with him clearly but kindly, and explain rather than demand.

Let me spin this around. Consider how well those other parenting methods work. How much time do they take? We usually find that power and control work in that moment, but as soon as you stop supervising, challenging behaviour returns. If smacking, for example, worked so well, we wouldn't have to keep doing it. Yet parents who smack (or use time-out) often find these strategies are relied on over and over again.

Recent Australian data from the Australian Child Maltreatment study shows that approximately 61 per cent of young people experienced corporal punishment (defined as being physically hit for discipline more than three times during childhood). Those who experienced corporal punishment were more likely to experience major clinical depressive disorder and generalised anxiety disorder than those weren't hit.[100]

According to Professor Darryl Higgins, being smacked as a child 'almost doubled the risk of mental health problems for young people up to age 24, and that finding is consistent with the broader literature on the effects of corporal punishment. There are no positive outcomes and there's a range of negative outcomes – and that's why we say to parents that it's never okay to hit your children.'

Other research shows that being smacked stops problematic behaviour briefly, but in over 70 per cent of cases, the child returns to that or similar challenging behaviour in less than 10 minutes! And while disciplinary approaches that emphasise control and restriction may not be as harmful, they're all externally oriented, meaning that children are behaving at the shallow end of the motivation continuum. Internalisation is hard when we play in that zone.

Do we always have to sit down and work things out together? No. It's neither reasonable nor practical. Instead, some other need-supportive responses will be helpful.

Giving your child in fantasy what they can't have in reality

Here's how this works: Imagine you're in the supermarket with your child. You're at the checkout and it's been a long tiring day. You just want to get out of there and get home. Suddenly your child pipes up, 'I want a lolly!' Inwardly you groan. It's right before dinner and you need to say no. You can feel a tantrum brewing. The last thing you want is a public meltdown! It doesn't have to end like that. Here's what you do.

First, connect with your child. Touch him on the arm, get down to his level and make eye contact. It's estimated that 90 per cent of good parenting is involved connection: helping your child feel seen, heard, and valued. Then, give him what he wants in fantasy. Say, 'I wish you could have a lolly! Wouldn't that be great? What kind would you get?' Hopefully your child will start to calm down straightaway, and think about the answer. 'Freddo Frog,' he might say. 'Oh that's a great choice. I'd pick a lollipop, or maybe freckles.'

Depending on how big your child's feelings are, you might need to extend the fantasy. You might say, 'What if our car was made of lollies? We'd never have to go to the supermarket again!' Your child might say, 'The wheels could be cookies!'

When you give your child what he wants in fantasy, it shows him that you understand his feelings and you care. Once he hears this, it's much easier for him to transition from overwhelmed by his big feelings to dealing with a situation that (from his perspective) is less than ideal.

When you engage your child in fantasy you're speaking to him in his favourite language – play. This reinforces your connection. It also shows your child that even if the world sometimes feels unfair, it's basically safe. This is because he's felt heard and understood. But does it work?

I received an email from Alex, a guy who sat sceptically in one of my workshops as I described this very principle one wet winter's night in Sydney. In the email he says, 'I had just taken my daughter to swimming lessons when I got a text from my wife asking me to grab a few things from the supermarket.' He responded breezily, 'No problem,' but as he got to the checkout, his daughter, Edie, asked for a lolly. Alex said no, and immediately the tears appeared.

He says in his email to me, 'Hang on, haven't I heard this scenario before? I crouch down and with soft eyes tell Edie that I like lollies too.' He asked her, 'What sort of lolly?' to which she replied, 'Red one.'

'Oh, I like red lollies too,' he said. 'I like green ones as well. Do you like green ones?' This continued as they paid for the groceries, and when they left Edie was calm and happily eating a banana. Alex says, 'I was already feeling pretty smug about this but then turn round to see the other parent and an old guy behind me in the queue giving me a round of applause.'

We might not always get a round of applause, but putting this principle into practice will help us through the tough 'no's' with our children. They may still want what they can't have, but we'll be able to playfully get them through it. And in the process, we teach them about limits and boundaries.

This approach works with children in the supermarket. And it works with teenagers who want to go to parties where alcohol will be served. It works, too, with tweens melting down because they really, really, really want to keep gaming or chatting with their friends on social media even though it's 9.30 at night and we're done! The process is simple:

1 Tell your child you can see exactly how they feel.

2 Empathise by saying, 'Don't you just wish that you could ...' or 'Wouldn't it be great if ...'

3 Embellish it if they're open to having some fun.

4 Reassure them that you wish they could enjoy that 'thing' too.

5 Restate your limit gently.

6 Wait for them to get it and move on.

Other simple things parents can do to guide their children are:

- Explain that you know it's a big deal but sometimes parents have to make the decisions, even when their kids don't like it. That this is reasonable, and in some cases it might even be a failure of parental responsibility not to do so.

- Use distraction so your child can regulate their emotions, and later on have the bigger conversations (when you both have time).

- Kick it down the road. Tell your child you understand that this is a big deal, but no one has the head space to deal with it perfectly right now. As a result, your decision as the parent stands, but the matter can be dealt with properly once everyone has the capacity to work through things the way we'd prefer.

This final point is particularly important. Often we feel that problems and challenges need to be addressed in the here and now. Decisions need to be made. Children need to be disciplined. Results need to be achieved. It's remarkable how many issues we can reduce to almost nothing with kindness, compassion, and intention, by giving everyone time to process things and determine better solutions. It isn't necessary to fix everything right now.

Furthermore, in the real world, this more considered style of conversation and parenting can easily blend into how you do things all the time. When the children need guidance, some simple questions work far better than command and control. Try these basic suggestions:

- It looks like things aren't going so well. Do I need to help out or are you okay?

- Everyone is really struggling here. It's a tough morning. What should we do to get things going a bit better?

- This is a tough scenario. What would you do if you were me?

- I know you're mad about this. How can I help?

- What would you want me to do if this was about your little sister/brother rather than you? If they were asking, what would you expect me to say?

These questions are shortcuts to empowerment. They're questions that give your child a voice that encourages wisdom and autonomy, and they tap into their sense of competence. They're also questions that show a level of trust in your child's ability to tune in to their values and make choices that point in a positive direction. Most important of all, asking questions like these reduces control but shows your child that you're unquestionably involved, expecting structures to be considered and followed, and supportive of their autonomy as much as you can be.

All of the common parenting questions I receive – about getting kids to do their chores, go to bed on time, treat their siblings nicely, stop being so defiant towards us; how to foster honesty; and even how hard we should push extracurricular activities – can be dealt with using the principles of need-supportive parenting. Even dealing with friendship challenges and bullying.

Belgian researchers Bart Soenens and Maarten Vansteenkiste teamed up with University of Rochester scholar Christopher Niemiec, to examine how autonomy supportive approaches affect relationships between our children and their friends. As you might expect by this stage of the book, parents who say 'no' in controlling ways in relation to their children's friendships turn those prohibited friendships into alluring 'forbidden fruit'. This research team found that the more restrictive parents were about who their children were friends with, the more likely it was that their children affiliated with what research psychologists call 'deviant' peers (which basically means kids who get up to mischief and antisocial behaviour). Force creates resistance. From the child's perspective, high levels of parental control hurt the parent/child relationship, undermine autonomy, and send a clear message to the child that the parent doesn't believe they're competent and capable of making wise friendship choices.

When parents try to control their child's friendship choices in a restrictive way, it drives the child in the very direction the parent is trying to stop. Merely saying, in a controlling manner, 'I don't want you playing with those kids' literally increases the likelihood that your children will play with precisely the peers you'd prefer they avoided. But when autonomy-supportive approaches are used, children are more likely to avoid 'deviant' peers and associate with prosocial peers. Parents who ask questions to explore a child's understanding of what a good relationship is and how they can support their child in healthy relationship decisions – need-supportive parents – have children who ultimately make better friendship choices.

When you have to say no

Now and then, you'll find that all of the need support in the world isn't getting you to a resolution that adult wisdom shows is necessary, and intervention is required. Getting this right, however, is tricky. There is benefit in children making mistakes and learning from them. But sometimes they don't learn. Other times, someone might be hurt. We must be discerning in identifying when to step in and when to stay out.

In many cases the stakes are low. For example, the kids are at each other. They're snappy and cheeky towards you. They're refusing to go to bed or turn off the screen. These are annoying challenges that create ructions in relationships, but they're a far cry from the more serious difficulties many parents face. High-stakes challenges could include children wanting to attend a party where you know there will be alcohol available. Or a teen pleading to go on an unsupervised road or camping trip with a group of other kids you don't know, and who might have intentions that are unsafe, unhealthy, and unwise.

In scenarios where the risk of harm is great or relationships are being jeopardised, parents have an obligation to be involved and potentially to increase the level of control they show. But once again, there are ways we can do this that minimise the controlling aspects of our interaction. In each of these scenarios, we can say no gently by giving our children in fantasy what they can't have in reality:

'You'd love to go to that party, wouldn't you? Everyone's going to be there and you feel like you're missing out. Wouldn't it be awesome if you could party every weekend? Don't you wish we weren't so strict sometimes?' This approach sets a clear standard. 'The answer is no. But ... I'm totally seeing the world through your eyes, kiddo. I love you and want good things for you, but I see why you want this, and it makes sense.'

The same process applies with the other scenarios I've suggested. 'You're so mad at me. Sometimes you wish I'd leave you alone so you could do whatever you wanted. That would be the best, wouldn't it? How much better would you feel if you were totally in charge of yourself? Or even the whole world! Amazing.' While this type of statement shows a child we see things from their perspective, it's also a gentle affirmation of rules and limits.

Even in such scenarios, though, we can still be involved and work towards creating structure and supporting autonomy. We might sit with our child and explore why this issue matters so much. Perhaps we'll explain our concerns and try to empower them. But when they dogmatically refuse to consider our suggestions and insist on doing things that go against our better judgment, it's okay for us to say, 'No, I won't allow this.' When we do, it's best to explain our reasons and ensure they understand. But – to be unambiguous about this – it's okay, and even important at times, to say no to our children.

As with everything related to need-supportive parenting, it's not so much what we say as how we say it. It matters too that we do what we can to minimise the extent to which we do say no.

17

When my child won't listen

Sometimes you can do EVERYTHING right. You can explore, explain, and empower. You can be involved, structured, and autonomy supportive. And ... things still aren't going to work out. Kids have to go their own way every now and again. When that happens, what can you fall back on? What are your options when your child simply won't listen? You're trying your hardest to facilitate an environment that supports autonomy, but it's like hitting your head against a brick wall. What then?

One of the most frequently asked questions I receive in my inbox goes something like this – how do I get my kids to listen?

This chapter has about 20 ideas to help. Hey, I know that's a lot: you've asked for a drink and, rather than a cup of water, I'm turning on the firehose! But first, as always, there's a bit of a story we need to get into.

I'm terrible with cold weather. Multiple layers of clothing are a burden. Frozen fingers make doing things like playing piano or opening a packet of biscuits tricky, and even the loving touch of my wife's cold fingers on my skin becomes an exquisite form of torture! The beach is my happy place; I live for the water, for that

Endless Summer. I hate the cold so much I've avoided *ever* going to the snow, much to my family's disappointment.

With this snippet of personal background, you can imagine my frustration on a cold midwinter's Sunday afternoon when my youngest daughter skipped out the front door and left it open.

I called out after my eight-year-old, 'Emilie, close the door please.'

Emilie ignored me. Oh, she heard me all right, but she purposefully chose to keep skipping towards her scooter without zero intention of turning around and shutting the door.

Despite the cold, I felt my temperature rise. With a deliberately stern face I strode to the door, stood in the tiled entry, and said loudly, 'Emilie, I asked you to do something. Now you come back here this instant and shut the front door.'

But she was gone. In those few seconds, my pathetic commands carried across the concrete driveway towards the kerb Emilie had just left, scooting to her friends, who were engaged in a perfect children's adventure in the park across the road.

Why kids won't listen

If you have a child who's a chronic non-listener, your first port of call is to rule out medical issues. A quick visit to the GP will give you the answers you need. Appointments for the doctor can be hard to book, though, and there's a level of expense many of us would rather do without. If that's you, then a cheaper test is to stand by the door and quietly ask who wants ice-cream (or who wants some money to go buy treats at the shop). If your child jumps up with an enthusiastic yes, your hearing test is probably complete.

Assuming there are no physiological issues, there are a host of other reasons our children won't listen. But the reality is that they can hear. They are listening. We're not speaking correctly when we complain that our children won't listen. Perhaps a better question might be: why don't our children do as they're asked?

As we consider our child's perspective, it's easy to identify countless reasons that they don't follow our instructions. These can include:

- Not wanting to be told what to do (which is probably a bit like us right?)

- A hyper-focus on what they're doing right now

- A preference to do something/anything other than what we're asking them to do

- Additional needs (like ADHD or autism)

- They're Hungry, Angry, Lonely, Tired, or Stressed (HALTS)

- The quality of our connection with them

- How many things they've already been asked to do

- The fact that their sibling isn't being asked to do the same thing

- Whether it's something they care about

- It's too early in the day

- It's too late in the day

- They're full

- They don't want to work with their sibling on a job

- They don't like the way we're asking them/telling them to do that thing

- Not actually having the skill or ability to do as they've been asked

- And so many more reasons …

In many cases, it's not just one thing but a combination of things. Being attuned to our children's capability and mental state can help us to understand when we should be asking, what we should be asking, and how we should be asking.

Yet sometimes things have to be done, regardless of how everyone feels. In those situations, we need compliance.

The compliance conundrum

These days compliance is a dirty word in the parenting blogosphere. For many people, compliance means that a parent is a demanding authoritarian, expecting children to follow orders regardless of any preferences they may have to do otherwise. Compliance connotes coercion and intrusiveness, which is not gentle.

As with every social media firestorm, there may be a kernel of truth to this. Compliance isn't a healthy long-term objective for our children and it isn't an ideal focus for our parenting.

But can we be real for just a minute?

They simply have to buckle up in the car. They should swim between the flags, wear shoes while riding a scooter, leave the cat alone, and stop throwing knives at their brother! These are safety issues. And they matter. The table does need to be cleared, the school bag put away, or the stinky sports gear placed in the laundry basket. It's called being part of the family and learning to do your part.

As I explained in Chapter 16, parents have an obligation to help children follow rules. It's how civil society operates. And while we're keeping it real, let's be honest and recognise that beyond those considerations, it's also convenient; sometimes in our overwhelmed parenting lives, we don't care that much about our kids' needs. We really do just want them to do as they're told and make life convenient, if only for this one moment. So what do we do when our kids 'won't listen' and it actually does matter?

They actually do listen

If you pause and do a small audit of how well your child listens, you might be pleasantly surprised. Unless you're interacting with a child who has Oppositional Defiant Disorder, you'll probably discover that your child does listen. Regularly. Consistently. And well. Often even your ODD, ADHD, ASD child listens more than you might realise.

So spend a few minutes considering when they listen and when they don't. You may find that things are going better than you thought. Then again, we all want to do things a little better. So let's consider seven simple ways to build and encourage listening –

and compliance. (And please note, I'll be emphasising respectful approaches where compliance isn't all about authority, control, command, and coercion.)

The basic answers

You'll typically find that a handful of standard answers permeate the Internet, TikTok, Instagram, and parenting advice books when it comes to this topic. Let's acknowledge them first, because they can be helpful.

Keep it simple

Short sentences are easier to process than long lectures. Keep your statements and requests simple, clear, and direct.

Get on your child's level

Making eye contact, smiling, and ensuring your child has heard you always improves the likelihood that your child will act.

Repeat it back

Ask your child to tell you what you told them. If you ask them to pick up the wet towels from the bathroom floor and they're not responsive, ask them, 'What did I say just then?' and wait for them to tell you. When they can repeat it back, you know they've listened, and they know you expect action.

Speak more quietly

When our children aren't listening, we have a tendency to elevate the volume. But remember, your child isn't deaf. Speaking louder (yelling) won't draw them to you and it's unlikely to encourage them to want to listen to you. Try speaking softly. They'll open their ears, lean in, and listen carefully.

Gentle touch

A soft pat on the arm, a squeeze or a hug, or an arm across the shoulder … these gentle touches can be enough to act as a circuit-breaker so your child can pay attention to what you're asking and help move things along.

Drop the don't

Say what you want. Instructions about what not to do (such as, 'Don't hit the stick against the wall') demand a lot of your child. It's an effort to redirect their energies. Now they have to stop doing the thing that's bothering you and figure out something else to do instead.

Find a way to say 'yes'

When you have to say 'no', spin it into a 'yes'. If you're asked, 'Can we stay at the park longer?' you can say, 'You bet. We'll have a longer stay at the park on the weekend when we come back with your friends.' If they plead, 'Can we please have ice-cream,' respond with 'You sure love ice-cream. We'll have ice-cream on Friday night with our movie, like always.' Your yes usually translates to a 'not now', but if you phrase it right, it goes down a treat.

You'll note that these seven strategies are designed to help you remain autonomy supportive. You're generally being involved, moving towards structure, and supporting children's voice and preferences where you can. But they're not the strongest demonstration of true autonomy supportive parenting. They're seven strategies for real life that will help you move things forward if you're stuck.

The truth is that they're all essentially built around what's convenient for us, just with an autonomy supportive flavour where we can squeeze it in. Their foundation is that stuff has to be done and the kids need to get with the program.

If we want to be better parents, the five suggestions in this next section will help us take it to a whole new level.

The fancier answers

Connect

When you ask your child to do something, consider the connection. Connection means feeling seen, heard, and valued. Do your children feel like you see them as more than a convenient way to get something done? Trying to command without connection – like yelling between rooms – is a lousy way to have your kids pay attention and usually won't lead to anything resembling compliance. (Note that it's not realistic to expect that you'll 'connect' every time something needs doing. But maybe we can connect more than we currently do?)

Timing

If your child is in the middle of something – anything – their listening and compliance will drop way down. This doesn't mean we shouldn't ask our children to be involved in helping when they're engaged in something of their own choosing. That's not realistic. But when we're sensitive to their priorities, things go better. Consider statements like, 'When that episode is done, please turn off the TV.' Or 'Once you've finished eating [or playing, or reading, or …] please take that bath.'

Capability

We expect too little of our children physically and we expect too much of our children emotionally. Demanding they 'calm down' or 'stop it' might be more than they can manage. But asking them to clear the table (or pick up their socks or close the door) will typically not be too much. Consider their developmental capability, emotionally and physically, before issuing edicts.

Context

Your child might be perfectly capable of going to bed on time most nights, but on a sleepover night (or during some other major event), the context changes. Demanding perfect behaviour at a funeral might make sense and be a sign of respect, but if they're grieving and confused, or if all of their cousins are there and they're excited, we might need to adjust our expectations. Requiring our children to listen to us the same way in every context is akin to expecting our children to act like robots. Be mindful of context.

Gentle reminders

Call your child by name. Look at them and quietly remind them of the issue that's requiring focus. The fewer words you use the better. Two or three is ideal. For example, 'Your bedroom', 'Your stinky socks', 'The dishes', and so on. Say please, and smile kindly.

The advanced answers

Over the years, I've used all of the suggestions and strategies above countless times with my six children. But as time, experience, and learning have all developed in me, I've come to prefer the following advanced strategies. These are strategies that:

- Build better connection

- Promote competence and capability in our children

- Facilitate autonomy and intrinsic motivation, and

- Make me feel like I'm a better parent (and person)

These advanced strategies aren't about making a modest attempt at being autonomy supportive. They're the real deal.

We're now moving into the deep end of the motivation continuum. And you can feel it in the way you interact with your child when you try these ones out.

Work on it together

Being told to go and carry out a task on your own can feel both isolating and punishing. Often the tasks we ask our children to complete can also feel overwhelming, even when the task is within their capability. This is because they have other priorities, they're tired, or they simply don't want to do it alone. Our children want to be in our world. They love spending time with us. When we say, 'Let's do this thing together', we create connection and respect. And we create shared moments that can become meaningful highlights to our day. From cleaning the room to washing the dishes (or the car!) our children's willingness to get stuff done increases enormously when we collaborate with them.

As a bonus hint, you'll often find that you don't need to do much while you're 'working together'. Sometimes simply being present, chatting, and offering gentle guidance (like humorously saying, 'What are the first three things you're going to put away in this catastrophe of a bedroom?') is enough to get them going.

Ask and wait

After you've asked your child to do something and they don't do it, how long do you wait before you ask again? Ten seconds? One minute? My suggestion: wait longer. Give it about five minutes. As long as there are no screens involved (which numb our children's consciences and their capacity for intrinsic motivation), waiting after you ask your child to join you in doing a task is a powerful way for them to tap in to their inner voice, listen, and respond.

Often (though not always) your child will feel that pang of conscience whispering to them that the best version of themselves really ought to be helping. And if you're involved in the task they've been asked to help with, the pull to help and be involved will be even more powerful.

Recall my experience with my children in the yard (from way back in Chapter 9). To recap, I realised a few minutes into the task that the kids could be helping. I called Lilli (aged 12) and Emilie (aged 8) to help. Lilli rolled her eyes but came over and got involved. Emilie decided this wasn't for her. Rather than becoming agitated, I focused on tidying up and on chatting with Lilli. Within 30 seconds Emilie decided to join us. Her conscience had processed the request, recognised that we were together, and identified that she wanted to be a part of what was happening. Once again, I emphasise that our kids want to be in our world. Connection, collaboration, and a sense of control will lead to better outcomes.

Stop praising your kids

I've written extensively about why we shouldn't praise our children in a previous book, *9 Ways to a Resilient Child*, and you can also find some ideas on my blog at happyfamilies.com.au. But one thing I didn't mention there is that praise essentially gives kids a quick and easy shot of dopamine, the 'feel-good' brain chemical. The trouble is that cheap dopamine becomes very expensive. The more our children come to rely on our external judgments about their behaviour, the less helpful our children will be, unless they're receiving more and more praise.

The eminent 19th-century American thinker Ralph Waldo Emerson austerely said, 'The reward for a thing well done is to have done it.' If your children help, don't give them the verbal equivalent of a doggy biscuit. To acknowledge them, say thanks. And let it be.

Consider your ratio of correction/direction vs connection

If you find yourself in a relationship with someone who always tells you what to do and when to do it and demands that you hurry up and do more or corrects you for doing it poorly – all the time – you'll probably avoid listening to them. You'd rather be listening to anyone else. We've covered that thoroughly in the pages of this book. But when someone who truly sees you and hears you and values you asks for your help, you're more inclined to listen and participate in what they've asked you to do.

Spend time with your children building relationships together, doing things together, and working out solutions together. Connection creates a desire for compliance far more than correction and direction.

Remember your children are illogical and irrational

Just accept it. The reason your child ignores you, screams at you, refuses to help, and behaves like a child is because … she is a child! When our expectations for our children's behaviour are congruent with our child's actual developmental reality, their tantrums and refusals make sense. This isn't about setting a low bar. It's not about accepting mediocrity. Rather, it's shifting our mindset to acknowledge that our children have limited capacity.

You wouldn't sit at a piano and expect to play a concerto if you hadn't had ample opportunity to learn, practise, and refine. To play well requires time, development, and learning. It's the same for our children. And just because they can do something one day doesn't mean they can do it every day. Tiredness, hunger, overwhelm, and all of those other things I've written about above can interfere with what they can do, and make them illogical and irrational.

Stop making life all about your kids

My final idea is on the provocative side. In the early chapters of this book I spoke about the intensification and fetishisation of parenting in the modern world. When we make life all about our children, they feel a level of expectation and entitlement. They anticipate that we're there to do more than simply support and guide them. We're there to serve them.

If we can teach them that life is better when they help others, think of others, engage with others, and live for others, we'll find they're more likely to help out willingly – and enjoy the opportunity.

A couple of bonus ideas

The ideas above are comprehensive. They encompass the simple and mundane through to the advanced and profound. But in all of these strategies, two other principles will often help:

1 Where you can, remember the element of need-supportive parenting that reinforces the value of offering a clear rationale for your requests. If your child understands the why of what you're asking, she's much more likely to comply, because the request makes sense.

2 Make it fun. While everything doesn't have to be fun, and life isn't always a circus, tasks, jobs, chores, and whatever else you might like to call them are always easier when they're enjoyable.

When Emilie chose not to respond to my request to shut the front door, I had all 20 of these alternatives at my disposal. I chose a different path. As Emilie scootered up the street to play, I chuckled to myself. I relished her delight in life. I savoured her voice carrying up the street to her friends as she called to them to say she was coming to play.

And then … I closed the door myself. And that's not really such a big deal.

18 How do we parent on the same page?

You've read the book. (Well, most of it, anyway.) You like what you're reading. It sounds hard. It's a departure from what you're used to hearing, and perhaps even what you're used to doing. But you're in. You want to support your children's basic psychological needs. You want to be involved in your children's life in supportive ways. You love the idea of developing structures with your children. And the concept of autonomy feels right. You know that the chances of your children internalising positive values and functional ways of being are vastly improved when you raise them in a need-supportive environment. You want to start a parenting revolution in your lounge room!

You just have one problem. Your spouse/partner isn't so keen. They think that 'there's no school like the old school.' They prefer the past or even the present to this projected future of parenting. And you're experiencing resistance. What do you do?

Just as our children have basic psychological needs that require support, so do adults. Grown-ups operate the same way. We flourish when we experience a need-supportive environment. Our motivation and wellbeing are diminished when those needs are frustrated. Therefore ... consider what lecturing and reprimanding your partner is going to do. First, it will make them feel incompetent. You're saying to them that you know more than them and they should listen to you. That feels horrible to them and promotes a defensive, closed stance. Second, it will make them feel forced into a corner and their autonomy will be diminished. No one wants to do something because someone else said they should. And third, your relationship will likely suffer as they see you as someone who bosses them around and makes them feel incapable.

Additionally, making critical comments to your partner/spouse about the way they parent not only tramples their basic psychological needs. It also feels, at times, like a slight against their entire family. To criticise your partner's parenting is to also potentially implicate his or her parents. After all, your partner is likely to be parenting the way she or he was parented. When you tell your partner to change course, you're asking that they reconsider everything they've been shown about parenting by their parents, casting a shadow on their practices. To rethink your family parenting strategy means acknowledging that your parents may not have done a brilliant job in meeting your basic psychological needs, and the same goes for your partner. This can be tough.

But two things can be true at once. Your parents (or your partner's parents) might have been punitive or permissive. It's possible they were controlling, left their children feeling incompetent, and ruptured relationships, *and* that they did the best they could do. Having that conversation is tricky. But it is important. It means acknowledging that you are who you are because of their best attempt at parenting, while recognising that you want to be better.

There's so much to work through that it's no surprise that sometimes people don't want to go there; they don't want to question how they were raised or consider that there might be a better way.

This doesn't mean we should give up on our partner. It does mean we have to find better ways to work through our issues. Therefore, my first suggestion is that you accept that your partner may not be open to change at all and be comfortable with that. So long as there is no abuse or harm, trust in their intrinsic desire to do things – including parenting – well. Then get on with being the most need-supportive parent *and* partner that you can be. Your example might be all it takes, given time.

Second, ensure your relationship is strong. The more they experience unconditional positive regard from you, combined with supportive involvement, the safer they'll feel with you. The warmth and nurture your connection offers will typically support their relatedness needs. They'll *want* to behave in ways that support and strengthen that connection further.

My third suggestion is to acknowledge and recognise the many positive ways your partner already does contribute to the wellbeing of your children. My guess is that they're awesome with most things, even if you don't agree with everything they do. Celebrate that. Work with what's working. Supporting competence needs is motivating. The more success experiences you have in your parenting roles, the more motivated you'll each be to invest more in them.

My fourth offering, unsurprisingly, relates to your spouse/partner's autonomy need. If we return to what autonomy support looks like, you'll ensure that you support their autonomy need through:

1 Encouraging choice and initiative by talking through problems together

2 Providing a clear rationale and explanation for your preferences and any requests you make

3 Recognising the feelings and perspectives of your partner

As with your children, this is best done by exploring what your partner wants, needs, and feels. This might include asking questions like, 'When that was happening with you and our child, what did you need? What did you get? How did it make you feel?' This third element of the autonomy supportive approach (considering the perspective of another) appears first here because it makes so much difference for someone to feel heard and understood. Moreover, it sets the foundation for your conversation to move forward. You're listening to understand before you start saying what you want. If you were to step forward and say in a commanding way, 'I'm sick of you yelling at the kids. It has to stop', chances are you'll promote division. But gently saying, 'That was another tough situation. This kid is getting trickier lately. What did I miss? What did you need? What was the outcome? How are you feeling?' – not all at once, pick and choose! – will promote openness, vulnerability, and conversation.

From here, moving deeper into the conversation with a discussion about what you've been trying or what values you want to instil is a logical next step. 'I'm sure you don't want a parenting lecture, but would you be okay if I shared something that's worked for me lately? I'm really trying to stay peaceful inside so I can be patient. It makes me feel better and it makes our family feel more functional.'

Your partner could be resistant to that. Perhaps you might share something like, 'When I was a kid my mum was always yelling and it crushed me. But we're both struggling and I'm seeing the same thing happen to our little one.' This soft but clear explanation of values in a warm and involved environment improves the likelihood of progress. It's a capacious way of saying, 'Here's where I'm at.' Or just a simple, 'I don't think we're on the same page with the way we're responding to challenges with the kids,' might be enough to prompt a conversation. Remember, though, NEVER start this conversation when emotions are high. Defensiveness and conflict (or stonewalling) will almost always result.

Last, we want to encourage autonomy in a need-supportive way. Perhaps we might ask our spouse/partner, 'How can we work on this? Where do we meet? How do we move forward?' The process is the same as it was for your three-year-old and your teenager. Support their needs.

Will it work?

Fast is slow. Slow is fast. It's unlikely you'll experience breathtaking change (with your children or another adult in your life) simply because you have a conversation that builds on this need-supportive process. That's not how this works! Internalisation takes time and practice. In the meantime you'll discover that, under pressure, you'll each fall back on your most practised habits. This is normal.

For the level of shift you're seeking, motivation has to be at the identified level of the motivation continuum (or better, but that takes time). That is, your partner has to believe in the value of the change in parenting behaviour. Without this there won't be any change. External and introjected motivation are only ever short-term. If the new behaviour is valued (identified), then over time and through practice, it will shift to integrated and even intrinsic.

Creating a need-supportive environment and being involved and setting expectations in need-supportive ways will become a part of who you and your partner are. You'll see challenging behaviour as an opportunity to check in with one another and your child, explore what's going on, and develop structures collaboratively to move through difficulties. Eventually need-supportive parenting will feel healthy, positive, and natural. It will have integrated to the point that it becomes intrinsic. It will be how you do it, because it feels right.

Of course, that's in a perfect world. If you're not living in one of those right now, your next best bet is to make your partner an offer. Ask if you can experiment together. Try it your partner's way for a week and then try it your way for a week. Ask questions about how it felt. Ask the children how they felt. Consider what felt helpful and what felt hurtful. Look for ways to integrate your learnings that feel positive and motivating for you.

The final option I suggest is that 'you do you' and let your partner do what's authentic for them. Sometimes you won't see eye to eye. This isn't an irreconcilable difference. As long as your children are safe, you can go on loving your partner in spite of the parenting style discrepancy. Your children will be fine. They'll learn how to navigate different relationships and different personalities. And who knows … perhaps over time your influence might even rub off on that impenetrable spouse of yours.

Parenting is about you – the parent. It's really not about your children at all. If it were about the children, perhaps it might be called *childrening*. Recall from our earliest chapters that parenting wasn't even a 'thing' until the 1970s. We're still figuring this out. Be patient with your partner. Keep learning together.

19

The parenting revolution

Parenting sometimes feels like a 1000-piece puzzle, all sky. But as you've worked your way through this book, I hope that it feels more manageable. I'm hoping that the concept of need-supportive parenting coupled with the pattern of compassionately exploring our children's worlds, explaining with clarity the *why* for our requests, expectations, and structures, and the collaborative empowerment we can develop with our children will feel intuitive and right, and that with practice, you'll find these approaches helpful in all of your relationships. The very best of current science points in this direction as the future of 'good' parenting.

Now and then, you'll still feel overwhelmed. You'll wonder what to do, where to turn, *how to be.* That's normal. Truth be told, we're all making it up as we go along. Now and then we find something that works for us, so we hang on to it. I believe that the things I've outlined here will, with practice, work for you.

In the introduction to this book I cited Dr Blaine Fowers and his statement on marriage. Let me return to that here. In speaking of the best marriages, he stated, 'I have become convinced that strong marriages are built on the virtues or character strengths of the spouses. In other words, the best way to have a good marriage is to be a good person.'

In the same way that our marriages and relationships become fuller and more resilient as the individuals in those relationships strive to cultivate virtues such as compassion, self-restraint, friendship, generosity, and forgiveness, our relationships with our children also thrive through the development of these virtues. We have those virtues inside of us. A need-supportive environment helps us access them, develop them, and live them. And our children have the seeds of those virtues inside them too. Our job is to provide that high-quality, need-supportive environment that will help them to access those same virtues, develop them, and live them – hopefully better than the way we've done it ourselves.

To parent this way requires more than just a supportive environment. We have to trust that these attributes are actually there, in us and our kids. Then we must give appropriate care and attention to develop these attributes. And we have to practise, because mistakes are guaranteed. Millions of them. Intentional and deliberate practice are essential for us to be better in our adult partnerships, but also in our relationships with our children. Here's the pain point: these attributes tend to be developed best at the times they're being most tried. Patience is an example of this. We don't really know that we have it until it's being tested to its utmost. When we fail to exercise patience (as your patience is being tried), we then have the opportunity to rehearse – to try again and do it better next time. It requires awareness, intention, and consistent commitment to the cause. That's what creates a revolution.

I recently began piano lessons. This is the first time I've deliberately attempted to play the piano since I was a teenager. As I learn new pieces, there are certain bars that are trickier than others. When I've stumbled over the notes, my teacher has asked me to go back to the place I lost momentum or made mistakes and play the notes slowly and carefully, ten times without error. It's this intentional and deliberate practice that's improving my piano. Our task, as parents, is to take a similar approach with our parenting. If we yell, we should pause and recognise we 'played that part poorly'. A heartfelt apology to our child followed by, 'Can I try that again without yelling?' will move you forward. Do it ten times without a mistake and you'll know you're becoming a better parent. The revolution continues.

And, in the same way that a teacher can point out flaws in our style at the piano – things that are in our blind spots – a child or partner might also be able to compassionately highlight what they've noticed. (At our invitation, of course: unsolicited advice tends to divide rather than repair and strengthen.)

It's powerful to see what happens when parents are their children's strongest supporters; the ones who believe in the competence of their child and encourage them to use their autonomy. As parents we stand on sacred ground with how we respond and react to the shortcomings and imperfections of our children. To watch a parent rally to their child's side and turn towards that child during a challenging and contentious moment rather than turn away; when a parent encourages rather than criticises; when they see the best in their child rather than the worst; and when they lift their child up rather than push their child down: these moments say so little about our child and so much about us. It's inspiring to see parents who turn towards their children with compassion, understanding, enthusiasm, and hope.

In this final chapter, I offer what I believe is the most important reason we should practise a need-supportive parenting style. It's one that relates to our children's voice.

Power corrupts

In October 2022, a small media storm was brewing in relation to calls for smacking children to be banned. The media thrives on these moments, although most of them, like this one, are forgotten within days of their commencement.

As is often the case, I received media enquiries and was invited to speak on many television and radio programmes about the issue. Parents and grandparents were up in arms defending their right to hit their children. 'This is why we've got a discipline problem!' they railed. 'Kids these days need someone to teach them to be respectful!' they furiously typed into the social media streams of news outlets, failing to see in their comments the irony that hitting someone is disrespectful.

In my interviews I outlined all of the reasons smacking doesn't work. I pointed to the more than five decades of studies failing to find a single redeeming factor in physical discipline. I outlined the logical arguments against this approach to correction. I suggested that discipline means 'to teach, guide, or instruct', or at least it did way back when Latin was the language of the day (and from which the word derives), and that punishment means 'to make someone pay a price; to exact retribution'. Etymological arguments were insufficient.

I spoke about the morally questionable concepts underpinning smacking, and the way it perpetuates a domestic violence narrative: that sometimes someone who loves you needs to hit you. When people said, 'You can't reason with a toddler', I pointed out that you can't reason with an 80-year-old with dementia either, and it wouldn't be right to hit them. The very thought is an affront to decency! I could go on and on with my arguments. In spite of my best efforts, a surprisingly high proportion of the Australian population remained stridently opposed to my position.

It wasn't until I sat with my wife, Kylie, and shared my profound sadness at the responses I'd heard, that something twigged. Kylie shared her experiences of being smacked as a child. She and her sisters were subject to severe physical punishments by a mother who meant well but knew no better, and who carried generations of trauma and pain.[101] Then my insightful wife made a comment. 'Because of the way I was raised, I never had a voice. And that's why, even now in my 40s, I'm only beginning to feel safe enough to express myself and tell you how I feel, what I need, and what I want.'

The way we're parented casts a long shadow that stretches into the remainder of our lives. Likewise, the way we parent our children casts a long shadow that stretches into the remainder of theirs.

And that, to me, is what this is really all about. It's the long view.

We can get caught up in the challenges of immediate compliance. Your six-year-old might refuse to brush his teeth. Every. Single. Night. Your children might fight or speak unkind words to one another. A lot. Perhaps you're dealing with sleepless nights and fussy eating. Teething. Or teen troubles and rebellion. In the immediacy of the moment, we feel compelled to act. We must fix this situation. We must teach our child. *They have to learn.* And in our rush to ensure that no teaching moment is ever lost, we dive in and start at them. We correct. We direct. We command. We control. Each time we do it, we shatter their self-perceptions of their already fragile competence. We cause splits and tears in the fabric of our relationship. And we deprive them of the opportunity to self-determine, reducing access to autonomy. In short, with the truest and best of intentions, we override their voice as we tell them – over and over again – what is expected, how it is expected, why it is expected, and that they're not living up to those expectations. In due course, the voice they hear inside their head becomes ours. What does that voice sound like?

When relatedness needs, competence needs, and autonomy needs are frustrated, that sweet voice our children possess is drowned out. Perhaps it's their angry and damaged voice, yelling at the world. More likely, as my wife described to me during our discussion, that voice is not even theirs. It's ours.

This is the reason that need-supportive parenting matters so much.

Whether we speak of smacking a child, using time out, withdrawing privileges, yelling, or any other parenting behaviour strategy so common in parenting today, each does the same thing. Each process uses parental power as an external demand on children. That power keeps our children from internalising their own values and morality, and prevents them developing the deep motivation they need to function optimally. But most of all, it silence their inner voice as we demand they listen to our more powerful one.

Need-supportive parenting does help in the moment. Of that, I am certain. This book shares just the smallest portion of the academic research demonstrating its value. My personal experience and the experience of thousands of parents who've tried these ideas attests to the practical application. It's less convenient and more taxing to practise. But it works.

The longer term, however, is where the real power of need-supportive parenting is seen. Children whose parents are involved and who support their relatedness needs feel valued and worthy. Children whose parents meet their competence needs through the offering of support and structure with scaffolding and working together on expectations and values believe in themselves. And children whose parents support their autonomy *find their voice*. They know they can speak and be heard. They know their voice counts for something. They know they can use their power to choose, to be volitional, to move mountains if they desire it.

What is a good parent? In so many ways, none of us are. We all fail miserably in our efforts to raise our children well. It is, as Freud suggested, an impossible task.

Yet, in so many other ways, *all* of us are good parents. We do the best we can with what we know. We invest. We are involved. We develop boundaries, structures, and expectations. We work hard at it. And we love. Oh, how we love.

Perhaps, more than anything, a good parent is one who gives a child, with loving structure, guidance, and support, their voice, and the trust and freedom to follow it.

For all that there is in this book pointing the way to being a paragon of parenting, and for all the usefulness practice provides, perhaps in times when we're stuck we might remember (and slightly amend) the advice of Dr Blaine Fowers: 'The best way to [be] a good [parent] is to be a good person.'

Acknowledgements

Thanks to the publishing team at ABC Books: Mary Rennie, Chris Kunz, Anne Reilly, and Rebecca Sutherland.

Additional thanks and recognition to Dr Renée Bazley for her evisceration of much of the text. Also gratitude for generous conversations with Prof. Wendy Grolnick, Assoc. Prof. Chris Niemiec, Prof. Todd Kashdan, and Prof. Wally Goddard.

Finally, thanks to Kylie and the kids: you're my proving ground and my inspiration.

Endnotes

Chapter 1 – The dark past of parenting

1   Blaffer Hrdy, Sarah, 'Liquid Assets: A Brief History of Wet-Nursing', *Natural History*, 12/95.

2   Cited in Traig, J., *Act Natural: A Cultural History of Misadventures in Parenting*, Ecco Press, New York, 2019.

3   Romanet, Emmanuelle, 'La mise en nourrice, une pratique répandue en France au XIXe siècle', *Transtext(e)s Transcultures*, 2013, 8, http: transtextes,revues.org/497; Blaffer Hrdy, op. cit. Her source for this extraordinary statistic is Lt Gen. Charles-Pierre LeNoir, head of the Paris police, whose job, she notes, was to monitor the referral bureaus used by parents to locate wet nurses.

4   See for instance Sussman, G.D., 'The Wet-Nursing Business in Nineteenth-Century France', *French Historical Studies*, 1975, 9, 304–28.

5   For more on this bizarre system, see Blaffer Hrdy, Sarah, *Mother Nature*, Pantheon Books, New York, 1999, pp. 351–70, to which my account is especially indebted; Shorter, Edward, *The Making of the Modern Family*, Basic Books, New York, 1975, pp. 176–89; and Colón & Colón, *A History of Children*, Greenwood Press, Westport, 2001, 326.

6   Snell, M., 'Surviving infancy in the middle ages' 2019, https://www.thoughtco.com/medieval-child-surviving-infancy-1789124.

7   Audin, J.M.V., *History of the Life, Works, and Doctrines of John Calvin*, Rev. John McGill (trans.), 1850, facsimile edn Wentworth Press, New York, 2019.

8   This quote and a host of references that support other information in this chapter is found at https://psychohistory.com/books/foundations-of-psychohistory/chapter-1-the-evolution-of-childhood/.

9   Hartley, L.P., *The Go-Between* (1st edn 1953), New York Review Books Classics, New York, 2002.

10　Rousseau did not write *Émile* as an advice book, but that is how many parents read it. To his credit, in the work Rousseau did condemn swaddling, promote breastfeeding and argue against wet nurses, suggesting that kids should be raised by their parents. Unfortunately, he was also big on the concept of 'hardening' children and exhorted parents to use fright masks, suggested that firing guns near children's heads would make them less anxious (!), discouraged education and books, and was a fan of children roaming naked in the woods. Subsequently, ice baths and exposure led to the premature and painful deaths of too many children whose parents thought Rousseau was on to something.

11　As quoted by Jennifer Szalai in, 'Raising Kids Isn't Easy. Parenting Advice Often Makes It Harder', *New York Times* online, 2 January 2019.

12　A brief detour here regarding Watson. While he is rightly recognised as a remarkably influential psychology thinker, his ideas were horrendously dangerous. Watson's disturbing view was that parents were the *least* qualified people to rear children due to the sentimental way they engaged with them. In his 1928 paper, 'Psychological Care of Infant and Child (archive.org/details/dli.ernet.7917) he stated, and I quote, 'It is a serious question in my mind whether there should be individual homes for children – or even whether children should know their own parents. There are undoubtedly much more scientific ways of bringing up children which will probably mean finer and happier children.' He advocated having a rotating cast of caretakers, changed every week to reduce attachment and dependence. And he suggested that, if a mother could not afford a nurse, she should pretend to be one when looking after the children so as not to be 'a sentimentalist masquerading under the name of "Mother."'

13　Watson, J. B., *Psychological care of infant and child*, New York, 1928, NY: Norton.

14　Watson advised, 'There is a sensible way of treating children ... Let your behaviour always be objective and kindly firm. Never hug and kiss them, never let them sit in your lap. If you must, kiss them once on the forehead when they say good night. Shake hands with them in the morning. Give them a pat on the head if they have made an extraordinarily good job of a difficult task. Try it out. In a week's time you will find how easy it is to be perfectly objective with your child and at the same time kindly. You will be utterly ashamed of the mawkish, sentimental way you have been handling it.'

15 Okorn, A., Verhoeven, M., & van Baar, A. 'The importance of mothers' and fathers' positive parenting for toddlers' and preschoolers' social emotional adjustment', *Parenting: Science and Practice*, 2021.

16 Roskam, I. & Mikolajczak, M., 'Gender differences in the nature, antecedents, and consequences of parental burnout', *Sex Roles*, 2020, 83, 485-498.

Chapter 2 – The 'impossible' profession

1 Kahneman, D., Krueger, A.B., Schkade, D.A., Schwartz, N. & Stone, A.A., 'A survey method for characterising daily life experience: the day reconstructions method', *Science*, 2004, 306, 1776-1770.

2 This was actually a headline in the *Sydney Morning Herald* way back in 2008. You can still find the article online at https://www.smh.com.au/national/happiness-is-not-having-the-children-20080509-gdscwh.html.

3 Twenge, J.M. Campbell, W.K., & Foster, C.A., 'Parenthood and marital satisfaction: A meta-analytic review', *Journal of Marriage and Family*, 2003, 65, 574-83.

4 Luhmann, M., Hofmann, W., Eid, M., & Lucas, R.E., 'Subjective well-being and adaptation to life events: A meta-analysis', *Journal of Personality and Social Psychology*, 2012, 102, 592-615.

5 Glenn, N.D. & McLanahan, S., 'The effects of offspring on the psychological wellbeing of older adults', *Journal of Marriage and Family*, 1981, 43, 409-421.

6 This data has been identified in a number of places, including this economic paper: https://warwick.ac.uk/fac/soc/economics/staff/ajoswald/revwellbeinginpanelsclarkosdec2002.pdf

7 de Montaigne, Michel, The Essays of Michel de Montaigne, trans., George B. Ives (New York, 1946), pp. 234, 516; Donald M. Frame, Montaigne: A Biography (New York, 1965), 3840, 95.

8   Important to note – he didn't specifically state parenting, but instead 'education of children', but it fits perfectly here and is close enough to what he said.

9   Freud, S., 'Analysis Terminable and Interminable, 1937.

10   https://www.vice.com/en/article/gqmx9j/here-lady-take-some-pills-for-your-hysteria-253.

11   Senior, Jennifer, All Joy and No Fun: The Paradox of Modern Parenthood, Ecco Press, New York, 2014.

12   Coulson, J.C., Oades, L.G., & Stoyles, G.J., 'Parents' subjective sense of calling in childrearing: Measurement, development and initial findings', The Journal of Positive Psychology, 2012, 7, 83–94.

13   For the academic nerd, feel free to read my entire doctoral research here: https://ro.uow.edu.au/cgi/viewcontent.cgi?referer=&httpsredir=1&article=4516&context=theses.

Chapter 3 – The ever-shifting goalposts of 'good' parenting

1   The Arbinger Institute (arbinger.com) are responsible for superb books on relationships, including The Anatomy of Peace and Leadership and Self Deception. I recommend them.

Chapter 4 – Modern parenting – a question of style

1   We will discuss Baumrind's ideas in detail in coming chapters. But a brief overview follows the Goldilocks principle. Some parents are a bit too hard (authoritarian). Some are a bit too soft (permissive). And some are just right (authoritative).

2   You can read all about it here: https://www.parents.com/parenting/moms/parenting-style-disney-princess-quiz/.

3   See https://www.beautythroughimperfection.com/hogwarts-house-says-parenting-style/.

4   None of these 'fad' parenting styles has any basis in science, including Myers-Briggs, but it's entertaining.

5   See https://karacarrero.com/myers-briggs-parenting-profiles/ as one example, though there are loads to be found.

6   https://www.weareteachers.com/jackhammer-parents.

7   https://www.newyorker.com/magazine/2022/10/17/helicopter-parents-are-last-years-model.

8   Because I'm an academic researcher by training, it pains me a little bit to talk about all of these 'non science-based' styles. But they're out there and people are talking about them, so I'm just going to hold my breath until the next chapters.

9   Note that I've used several terms in each characterisation. This will make sense later in the book as we explore critically important parenting styles from Baumrind and others. The first characteristic in each of the three dimensions is based on Schaefer's work (accepting, firm, autonomy supportive). The second is based on Baumrind's parenting styles (responsiveness, demandingness, autonomy supportive). The third is based on the work of Edward Deci and Richard Ryan, and is called autonomy supportive parenting (involvement, structure, autonomy support). The differences are nuanced and will be explored later in the book.

10 https://medicine.umich.edu/dept/pediatrics/news/archive/201907/failure-launch-parents-are-barriers-teen-independence.

11 For a handful of excellent academic resources on the topic see:
    Kouros, C.D., Pruitt, M.M., Ekas, N.V., Kiriaki, R., & Sunderland, M., 'Helicopter parenting, autonomy support, and college students' mental health and well-being: The moderating role of sex and ethnicity', *Journal of Child and Family Studies,* 2017, 26, 939–49.
    Kuppens, S., & Ceulemans, E., 'Parenting styles: A closer look at a well-known concept', *Journal of Child and Family Studies,* 2019, 28, 168-181.
    Padilla-Walker, L.M., & Nelson, L.J., 'Black hawk down?: Establishing helicopter parenting as a distinct construct from other forms of parental control during emerging adulthood', *Journal of Adolescence,* 2012, 3, 1177–90.

12 Lindke, C.A., & Oppenheimer, D.M., 'Hovering at the polls: Do helicopter parents prefer paternalistic political policies?', *Journal of Experimental Psychology: General.* Advance online publication, 2022.

13 Chamberlin, J., 'Tiger parenting doesn't create child prodigies', *Journal of the American Psychological Association,* 2013, 44. https://www.apa.org/monitor/2013/09/tiger-parenting.

See also Kim, S.Y., Wang, Y., Orozco-Lapray, D., Shen, Y., & Murtuza, M., 'Does "tiger parenting" exist? Parenting profiles of Chinese Americans and adolescent developmental outcomes', *Asian American Journal of Psychology, 2013, 4*, 7–18.

14   https://www.freerangekids.com/nancy-nord-on-common-sense-and-imaginary-dangers/.

15   This article via the ABC gives an accessible overview of why free-range parenting is associated with positive outcomes: https://www.abc.net.au/news/2016-04-07/sharman-free-range-kids-could-become-healthier,-happier-adults/7306740.

16   A detailed and informal look at this style of parenting, including an interview with Sroufe, is available at https://greatergood.berkeley.edu/article/item/why_attachment_parenting_is_not_the_same_as_secure_attachment.

17   Tronick, E.Z., & Gianino, A., 'Interactive mismatch and repair: Challenges to the coping infant', *Zero to Three*, 1986, 6, 1–6.

18   For all of the research from the Minnesota Longitudinal Study of Risk and Adaptation, see here: https://innovation.umn.edu/parent-child/publications/attachment/.

Chapter 5 – Is this the kind of parent I am?

1   Robinson, C.C., Mandleco, B., Olsen, S.F., & Hart, C.H., 'The Parenting Styles and Dimensions Questionnaire (PSDQ)', in B.F. Perlmutter, J. Touliatos, & G.W. Holden (eds), *Handbook of family measurement techniques: Vol. 3. Instruments & index*, Sage, Thousand Oaks, 2001, 319–21.

2   Professor John M. Gottman has a parenting style questionnaire that is unrelated to the Baumrind model of parenting and is available in his book, *Raising an Emotionally Intelligent Child*, Simon & Schuster, New York, 1998. It's probably the only other well regarded measure of parenting style in the world.

3   Gratitude to Professor Craig Hart, who kindly granted permission for me to use his parenting styles questionnaire in this book.

4   There are dozens, if not hundreds, of studies that summarise these
parenting styles and correlates. Rather than providing expansive lists
of articles that the typical reader is unlikely to review, I point scholarly
readers to Larzelere, R.E., Morris, A.S., & Harrist, A.W., *Authoritative
parenting: Synthesizing nurturance and discipline for optimal child
development*, American Psychological Association, Washington DC, 2013.

5   Grant, A., *Think Again: The Power of Knowing What You Don't Know*,
WH Allen, London, 2021.

Chapter 6 – Children's basic psychological needs

1   https://quillette.com/2022/08/17/why-i-left-academia-since-youre-
wondering/.

2   As a fascinating tangent, in *Don't Trust Your Gut* (Bloomsbury,
London, 2022) by former Google data analyst, Seth Stephens-
Davidowitz, the author points to big data from the United States
indicating that the suburb (so the literal environment) we choose to
raise our children in has a significant impact on their life outcomes,
including financially. He says the 'three big predictors that a
neighbourhood will increase a child's success are (i) Percent of residents
who are college graduates, (ii) percent of two-parent households,
and (iii) percent of people who return their census forms.' My sense
of why this is: parents who can afford to live in these suburbs are
conscientious. And they intuitively know that their children's needs
will be supported in these environments.

3   Women were rarely included in studies at all. Even medical textbooks
were written and built around the male anatomy.

4   Technically these participants were in the 'Glueck Study', but ultimately
their data was included in the 'Grant Study' and contributed to the
overall findings of the research.

5   JFK's data has been sealed until 2040.

6   Mineo, L., 'Good genes are nice, but joy is better', *Harvard Gazette*,
2017, https://news.harvard.edu/gazette/story/2017/04/over-nearly-80-
years-harvard-study-has-been-showing-how-to-live-a-healthy-and-happy-
life/.

7   This table is based on Ryan, R.M., & Deci, E.L., 'Self-determination theory and the facilitation of intrinsic motivation, social development, and wellbeing', *American Psychologist*, 2000, 55, 68–78.

Chapter 7 – Need-supportive parenting

1   I know, it's a terrible name. It's not catchy like 'gentle' or 'helicopter' or 'tiger'. The researchers behind need-supportive parenting never gave it a name. I did … and unfortunately I didn't major in marketing. It's the best I've got.

2   Ryan, R.M., Deci, E.L., Grolnick, W.S., & La Guardia, J.G., 'The significance of autonomy and autonomy support in psychological development and psychopathology', in Cicchetti, D., & Cohen, D., (eds) *Developmental psychopathology: Theory and method*, 3rd ed., Wiley, New York, 2016, 385-348.

3   Assor, A., Roth, G., & Deci. E.L., 'The emotional costs of parents' conditional regard: A self-determination theory analysis', *Journal of Personality*, 2004, 72, 47–88.

4   Roth et al. (2009) looked at positive conditional regard versus negative conditional regard and found that positive conditional regard (love and praise) is also damaging. When children think they're only 'good' when they do what we say, they experience conditional regard and it is detrimental, even when positively focused. Our kids are worthy because they're people. Full stop.

5   Grolnick, W., Frodi, A., & Bridges, L., 'Maternal control style and the mastery motivation of one-year-olds', *Infant Mental Health Journal*, 1984, 5, 72-82

6   Deci, E.L., Driver, R.E., Hotchkiss, L., Robbins, R.J., & Wilson, I.M., 'The relation of mothers' controlling vocalizations to children's intrinsic motivation', *Journal of Experimental Child Psychology, 1993, 55*, 151–162.

7   Van der Bruggen, C.O., Stams, G.J.J.M., & Bögels, S.M., 'Research review: the relation between child and parent anxiety and parental control: A meta-analytic review', *Journal of Child Psychology and Psychiatry*, 2008, 49, 1257–1269.

8   Collishaw, S., Gardner, F., Maughan, B., Scott, J., & Pickles, A.,

'Do historical changes in parent–child relationships explain increases in youth conduct problems?', *The Journal of Abnormal Child Psychology*, 2012, 40, 119–132.

9   Vasquez, A.C., Patall, E.A., Fong, C.J., Corrigan, A.S., & Pine, L., 'Parent autonomy support, academic achievement, and psychosocial functioning: A meta-analysis of research', *Educational Psychology Review*, 2016, 28, 605–644.

10   Bindman, S.W., Pomerantz, E.M., & Roisman, G.I., 'Do Children's Executive Functions Account for Associations Between Early Autonomy-Supportive Parenting and Achievement Through High School?', *Journal of educational psychology*, 2015, 107, 756–770.

11   Guay, F., Boggiano, A.K., & Vallerand, R.J., 'Autonomy Support, Intrinsic Motivation, and Perceived Competence: Conceptual and Empirical Linkages', *Personality and Social Psychology Bulletin*, 2001, 27(6), 643–650. See also Reed, K., Duncan, J.M., Lucier-Greer, M., Fixelle, C., & Ferraro, A.J. (2016), 'Helicopter parenting and emerging adult self-efficacy: Implications for mental and physical health', *Journal of Child and Family Studies*, 25, 3136–3149. Harvey, B., Stack, D.M., & Serbin, L.A., 'Contextual specificity in the relationship between maternal autonomy support and children's socio-emotional development: A longitudinal study from preschool to preadolescence', *Journal of Youth and Adolescence*, 2015, 44, 1528–1541.See also Brenning, K., Soenens, B., Van Petegem, S., & Vansteenkiste, M., 'Perceived maternal autonomy support and early adolescent emotion regulation: A longitudinal study', *Social Development*, 2015, 24, 561-578.

12   For a full treatment, see Deci E.L., & Ryan, R.M., *Self Determination Theory*, The Guildford Press, New York, 2017.

13   Joussemet, M., Koestner, R., Lekes, N., & Landry, R., 'A longitudinal study of the relationship of maternal autonomy support to children's adjustment and achievement in school'. *Journal of Personality*, 2005, 73, 1215-1236, and Deci, E. L., & Ryan, R. M. 'The "What" and "Why" of goal pursuits: Human needs and the self-determination of behavior'. *Psychological Inquiry*, 2000, 11, 227-268.

14   Neubauer, A.B., Schmidt, A., Kramer, A.C., & Schmiedek, F., 'A little autonomy support goes a long way: Daily autonomy supportive parenting, child wellbeing, parental need fulfillment, and change in child, family, and parent adjustment across the adaptation to the Covid-19 pandemic', *Child Development*, 2021, 92, 1679-1697.

Chapter 8 – The how-to's of healthy parental involvement

1   Maslow would go on to change psychology forever, studying the concept of self-actualisation and developing the famous 'Maslow's Hierarchy of Needs'.

2   For a fascinating, broad-ranging, and expansive overview of this and much more of Harlow's research and thinking, this original source, which is available free online, will be useful: Harlow, H.F., 'The nature of love', *American Psychologist*, 1958, 13, 673–85. http://psychclassics. yorku.ca/Harlow/love.htm.

3   Ardiel, E.L., & Rankin, C.H., 'The importance of touch in development', *Paediatrics and Child Health*, 2010, 15, 153–56.

4   Vagal tone is how we describe the activity of the vagus nerve, which is responsible for the regulation of internal organ functions, including heart rate, respiration, and digestion.

5   Sheldon, K.M., Kashdan, T.B., & Steger, M.F. (eds), *Designing positive psychology: Taking stock and moving forward*, Oxford University Press, New York, 2011.

6   Day, R.D., & Padilla-Walker, L., 'Mother and father connectedness and involvement during early adolescence', *Journal of Family Psychology*, 2009, 23, 900–04.

7   Personal communication via Zoom.

Chapter 9 – How to create structure that supports a child

1   Grolnick, W.S., Raftery-Helmer, J.N., Marbell, K.N., Flamm, E.S., Cardemil, E.V., & Sanchez, M., 'Parental provision of structure: Implementation and correlates in three dimensions', *Merrill-Palmer Quarterly*, 2014, 60, 355–84.

2   This quote is borrowed from Brown's popular animated YouTube
        video on the topic of empathy: https://www.youtube.com/
        watch?v=1Evwgu369Jw.

3   Shulman, E.P., Harden, K.P., Chein, J.M., & Steinberg, L., 'Sex differences
        in the developmental trajectories of impulse control and sensation-
        seeking from early adolescence to early adulthood', *Journal of Youth and
        Adolescence*, 2015, 44, 1–17.

4   Bru, E., Virtanen, T., Kjetilstad., V., & Niemiec, C.P., 'Gender
        differences in the strength of association between perceived support
        from teachers and student engagement', *Scandinavian Journal of
        Educational Research*, 2021, 65, 153–68.

Chapter 10 – The most powerful question in the world

1   Koestner, R., Ryan, R.M., Bernieri, F.J., & Holt, K.D., 'Setting
        limits on children's behavior: The differential effects of controlling vs.
        informational styles on intrinsic motivation and creativity', *Journal of
        Personality*, 1984, 52, 233-248.

2   Quote taken from Deci E.L., & Ryan, R.M., *Self Determination Theory*,
        Guildford Press, New York, 2017, p 8.

3   This 'working with' versus 'doing to' distinction was popularised by
        Alfie Kohn in his book, *Punished by Rewards*, Houghton Mifflin,
        Boston, 1993.

4   These activities are *not* a problem in and of themselves. In fact, a lot of
        research emphasises their value for enriching our children's lives and
        supporting them in other areas of life as well. But the reasons they are
        enrolled matter. Children's interests and preferences must be at the heart
        of these choices – and not just so that they can please their parents.
        Intrinsic motives make for better outcomes.

5   Borra, C., Iacovou, M., & Sevilla, A., 'New evidence on breastfeeding
        and postpartum depression: The importance of understanding women's
        intentions', Maternal and Child Health Journal, 2015, 19, 897-907.

6   Soenens, B., & Vansteenkiste, M. 'A theoretical upgrade of the concept
        of parental psychological control: Proposing new insights on the basis of
        self-determination theory', Developmental Review, 2010, 30, 74-99.

7   A fascinating and brilliant book by Jennifer Verdolin, *Raised by Animals* (Affirm Press, Melbourne, 2017), shows just how much animals trust that their young will develop healthily.

8   Landry, R., Whipple, N., Mageau, G., Joussemet, M., Koestner, R., DiDi, L., Gingras, I., Bernier, A., & Haga, S.M., 'Trust in organismic development, autonomy support, and adaptation among mothers and their children' *Motivation and Emotion*, 2008, 32, 173-188.

9   An important aside: I love my daughter. I love who she is and what she is achieving in her life. I am proud of her, and I'm grateful for her. Unconditionally. Unequivocally.

Chapter 11 – Complex needs

1   Data from https://www.aihw.gov.au/reports/children-youth/australias-children/contents/health/children-mental-illness.

2   Data from https://www.aihw.gov.au/reports/children-youth/mental-illness.

Chapter 12 – School refusal

1   At the time of writing, the government was launching an inquiry into the reasons for this increase. An accessible article describing more about school refusal can be found at https://www.afr.com/work-and-careers/education/absenteeism-on-the-rise-amid-falling-school-performance-20220920-p5bjey.

Chapter 14 – How to get my kids to do their homework?

1   You can find the entire inquiry here: https://www.parliament.vic.gov.au/images/stories/committees/etc/Homework_Inquiry/TOR_HVS.pdf.

Chapter 15 – How do I manage screens and kids?

1   You can read the entire article here: https://www.nytimes.com/2022/10/02/opinion/video-game-addiction.html.

2   Find details of the experiment here: https://dl.acm.org/.

Chapter 17 – When my child won't listen

1   A full overview is available here: https://www.australianchildmaltreatmentstudy.org/.

Chapter 19 – The parenting revolution

1   Kylie's mother has grown through that pain and has shared her deep regret for those actions as a parent.